D1798133

£3-50

More Performing Toys

More Performing Toys

Alice White

MILLS & BOON London

TAPLINGER PUBLISHING COMPANY New York

First Published Great Britain 1972 by Mills & Boon Limited,
17–19 Foley Street, London WIA IDR.

First Published 1972 in the United States by Taplinger
Publishing Co. Inc., 200 Park Avenue South, New York,
NY 10003, USA.

Copyright © Alice V. White 1972

British ISBN 0 263.05153.6
American ISBN 0–8008–5357–1

Library of Congress Catalog Card Number 72–2188

Made & Printed by Offset in Great Britain by
William Clowes & Sons, Limited
London, Beccles and Colchester

Contents

Note to American Readers

The following terms may be unfamiliar to some American readers and are accordingly clarified to facilitate the use of this book.

Lead shot	heavy metal disc
Plasticene	plastic clay
Sellotape	scotch tape or masking tape
Torch bulb	flashlight bulb
Torch battery	flashlight battery

Introduction

When I wrote *Performing Toys* I realised there was a great deal of pleasure to be obtained by creating weird and wonderful creatures which could perform a wide range of movements and sounds. But I never realised what a large number of people would find endless pleasure in the book.

All who have seen the children on television discovered that they really did enjoy making their puppets perform.

In the present book I have been able to show how a great variety of jointed creatures can be made from the throw-away junk which is to be found in every home. There is a greater variety of colour in waste materials nowadays and therefore paint need not be used so much as in the past.

In this book sounds do not play such an important part as the movements which can be obtained from some of the creatures. I have also added ideas for puppets made from fabric, because if one is to do drama about the planets, one must have earth people dressed in everyday fabrics.

Through the great interest shown in space projects these days, children are more aware of these ideas, and some of the creatures can even be electrified.

The link with English and Drama is very strong and a few poems have been selected from the work done by the second- and third-year children of Clint Road Junior School, Boys' Department, Liverpool (this is an E.P.A. School). My colleague, Ian Sharp, has once again contributed a section on performance.

Tools and equipment

Scissors Pointed, with 3-in. (8-cm.) blade.

Bradawl Wooden handle and sharp metal point, used for piercing holes in bottle tops, Fig. 1.

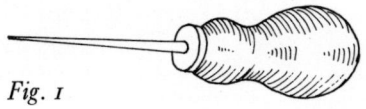

Fig. 1

Skewer Metal skewer is useful for burning holes in plastic containers.

Night light A night-light is useful for heating the skewer. (Always keep it in a metal container—a small tin.)

Needles Large-eyed, 2–3 in. (5–6 cm.) long.

Paste Brush With 1-in. (3-cm.) bristles.

Paste Use powdered paste (wallpaper type) but make up very thickly to a stiff jelly and keep in a screw-top jar. Use for sticking paper to balloons.

Adhesive Obtainable in tubes. Use for sticking sections of puppets together. Copydex, Bostik, Evo-Stik were used for puppets in this book, but virtually any good adhesive will suffice. (Elmer's Glue-all is suggested for the USA.)

String Must be thin. Alternatively, use book-binders' linen thread. Use for threading various sections of puppets together.

Thread Dark-coloured, but must be very strong. Use for suspending puppets from rods when performing.

Paint Cans of spray paint may be used. Follow the instructions on the can carefully.

How to make holes in plastic containers:
Heat a long needle or skewer in the flame of a night light or other form of heat. Push the heated needle through the plastic to melt a hole.

9

Materials

Almost any form of waste material can be used for puppet construction. Care should be taken to sort out thoroughly items of certain colours and shapes. For instance, Red-Lek (page 74) was made from red bottle tops and red containers.

If waste materials are carefully selected, then it may not be necessary to paint the finished puppet, or perhaps only part of it. Luna-Mog has most delightful yellow feet and white legs (all bottle tops).

The puppets in this book were made from the following:
Egg-box and egg-tray sections. Eggs delivered to shops are often on trays, but more usually they are in boxes of six, Figs. 2, 3 and 4. Here there is a wide choice, so look around and find different designs. Figs. 2b, 3b and 4b show how the sections look after they have been cut off from the main box.

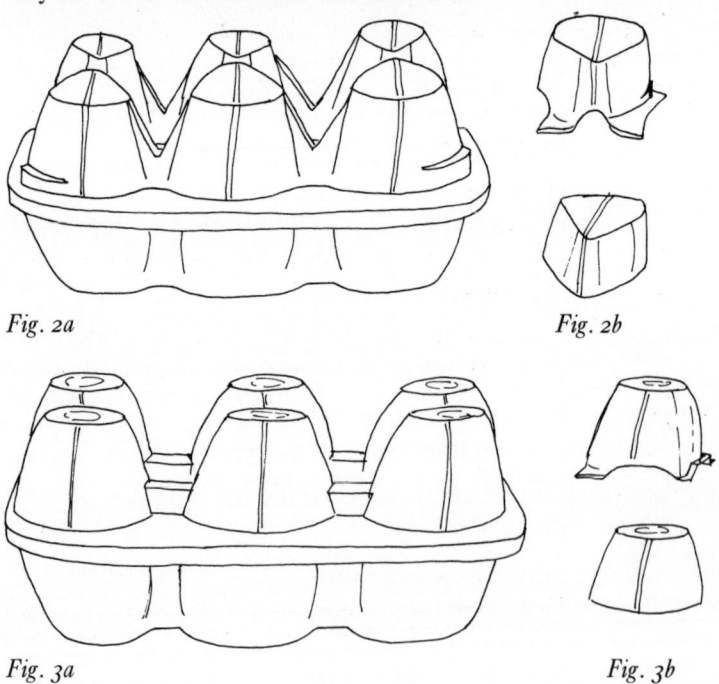

Fig. 2a   Fig. 2b

Fig. 3a   Fig. 3b

Fig. 4a   Fig. 4b

Plastic containers which have contained cream, yogurt, cheese, detergents, margarine, etc.

Cardboard tubes from toilet rolls, etc.

Bottle-tops, metal crown caps, plastic caps from all kinds of containers: aerosols, cosmetic and detergent containers, toothpaste tubes, etc. The tops may be very large or very small, and could include plastic lids from containers. A careful look at the diagrams will always show what kind of top is being used.

Paper beakers, or styrofoam coffee cups.

Balloons of all shapes and sizes.

Pipe Cleaners.

Buttons and beads of all shapes and sizes are useful for spacing out sections or making eyes.

Polystyrene spheres obtainable from handicraft centres or scientific warehouses. Used for heads. Make a hole through the centre with a long needle or thin wire.

Oli-Lek

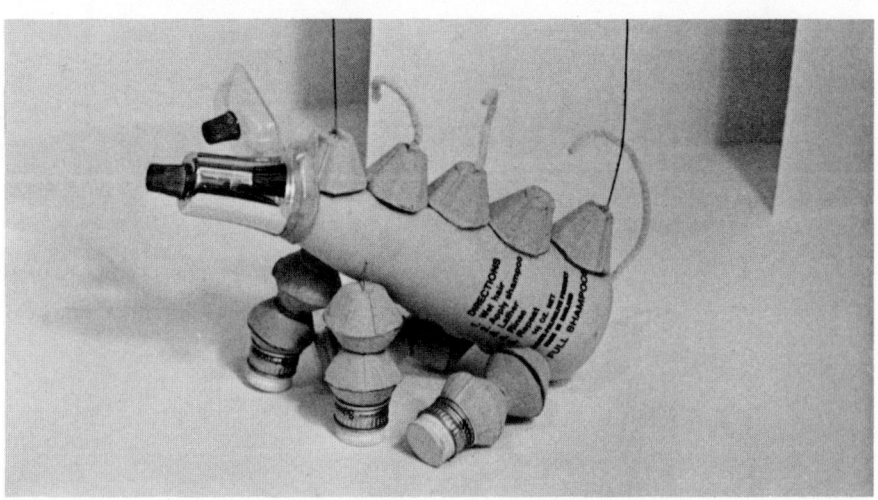

Materials required See Fig. 5. Four lengths of thread each 14 in. (35 cm.) long.

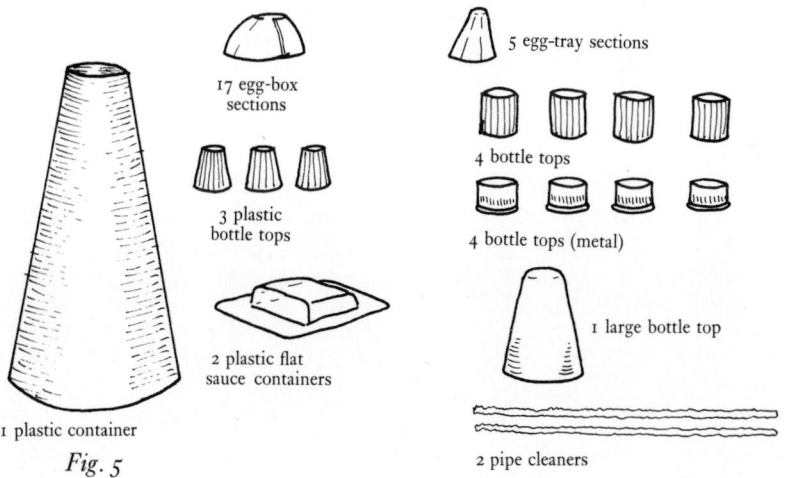

17 egg-box sections

5 egg-tray sections

3 plastic bottle tops

4 bottle tops

4 bottle tops (metal)

2 plastic flat sauce containers

1 large bottle top

1 plastic container

2 pipe cleaners

Fig. 5

To make

Legs   1. Make large knot on end of thread and thread on a bottle top, Fig. 6a, then add another one, Fig. 6b.

2. Thread on two egg-box sections and glue together, Fig. 6c and d.

3. Thread on two more egg-box sections and glue together so that the whole leg is rigid, Fig. 6e.

Make four legs like this.

Head and body Make holes in body for legs as for Ji-Lek and attach legs as for Ji-Lek (see page 28).

1. Stick five egg-tray sections across top of body as in Fig. 7.

2. Stick one egg-box section to neck of container and add a large bottle top, then a smaller one, securing all with adhesive, Fig. 8.

3. Make a hole in rear of container and stick end of pipe cleaner through. Bend to form a tail.

4. Cut other pipe cleaner in half and push through egg-tray sections on the spine and bend slightly.

5. Stick bottle tops on to plastic sauce containers and attach these sections to head. It may be necessary to use Sellotape for this, Figs. 9 and 10.

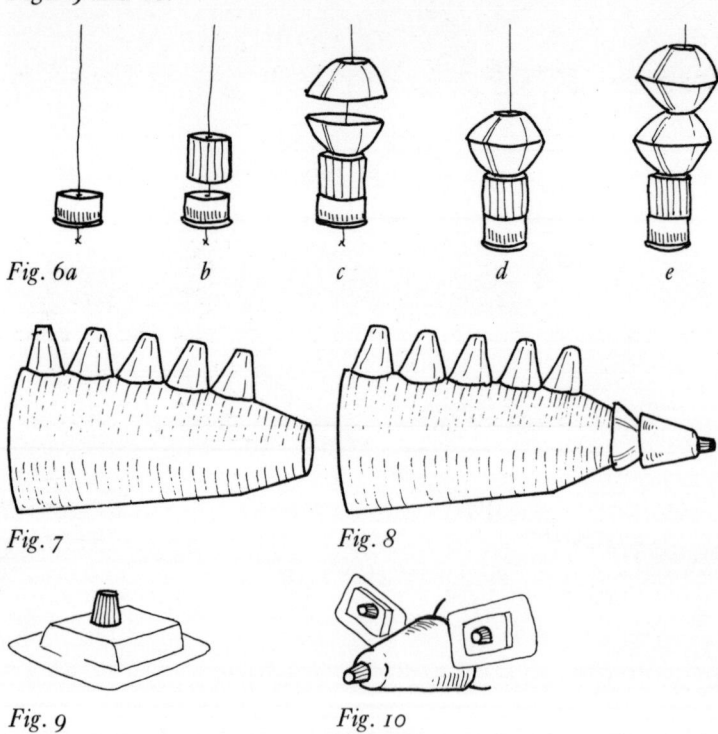

Fig. 6a   b   c   d   e

Fig. 7

Fig. 8

Fig. 9

Fig. 10

Fig. 11

15

Luna-Hog

Luna-Hog is really a delightful creature, with a facial expression which is most appealing.

Materials required
See Fig. 12. Eight lengths of thread each 8 in. (20 cm.) long.

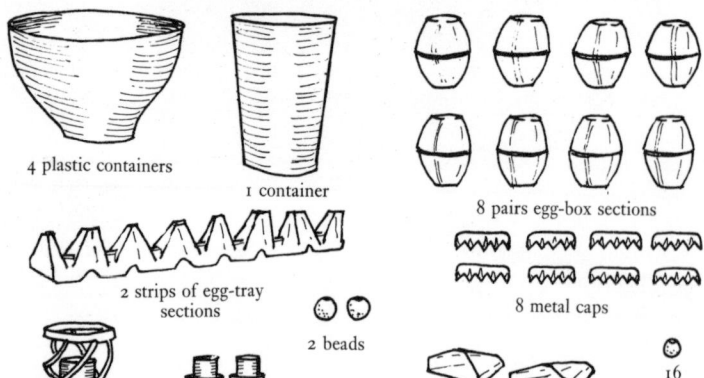

4 plastic containers

1 container

8 pairs egg-box sections

2 strips of egg-tray sections

8 metal caps

2 beads

1 bottle top

2 bottle tops

2 egg-tray sections

16 beads

Fig. 12

To make 1. Put knot in end of thread and thread on a bottle cap and a pair of egg-box sections, Fig. 13a.
2. Stick the egg-box sections to the bottle cap and thread on two beads. This completes one leg, Fig. 13b. Make eight legs in all.
3. Make two holes in each of the four plastic containers, Fig. 14.
4. Thread through the leg threads and tie, Fig. 15.
5. Stick the plastic containers together and make sure all legs are in the correct position, Fig. 16.
6. Stick on strips of egg-tray sections to hide the two joins of containers, Fig. 17.
7. Attach head and features, following the silhouette illustration, Fig. 18.
8. Make two holes in the rear and attach thread for suspending.

Also attach thread to the head.

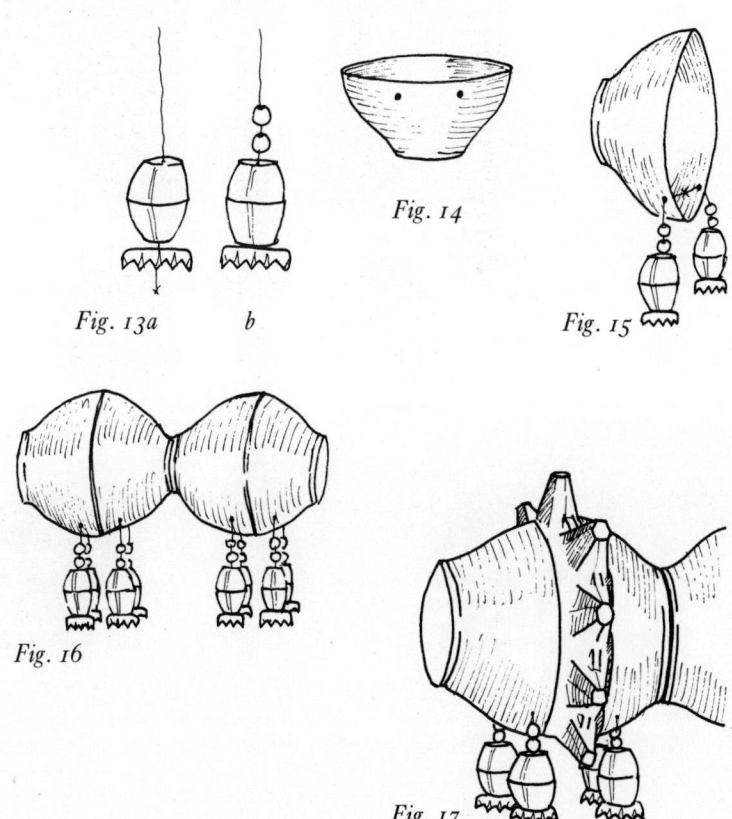

Fig. 13a   b

Fig. 14

Fig. 15

Fig. 16

Fig. 17

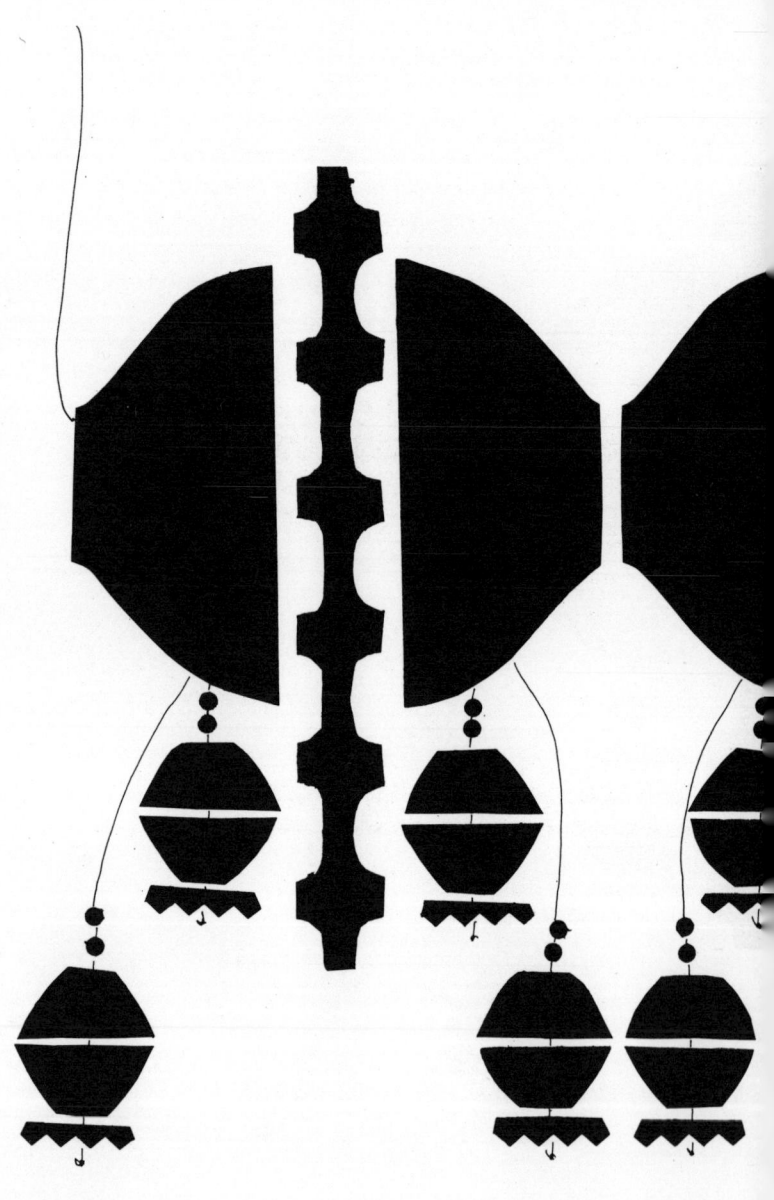

Fig. 18

18

Aero-Lek

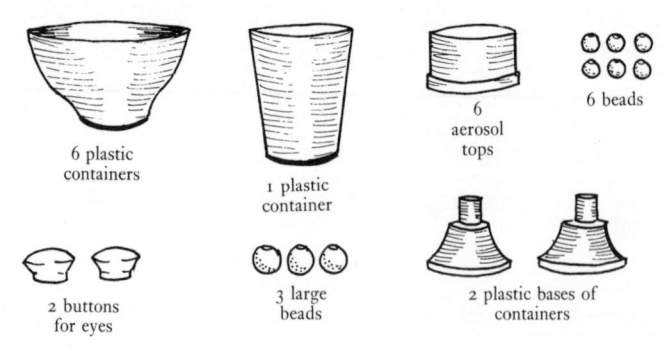

Materials required See Fig. 19. Six lengths of thread 12 in. (30 cm.) long. One length of thread 36 in. (90 cm.) long.

6 plastic containers

1 plastic container

6 aerosol tops

6 beads

2 buttons for eyes

3 large beads

2 plastic bases of containers

Fig. 19

To make   Make holes in the centre of all plastic containers and the six large tops.

1. Make two holes in one plastic container for legs, Fig. 20. Do the same with two of the other containers.
2. Make large knot in one of the shorter lengths of thread and pass through a large top and bead, Fig. 21. Repeat this for the six legs.
3. Thread each leg thread through a plastic container and tie securely, Fig. 22. Do this to the other two containers.
4. Make a knot in the long length of thread and pass through the first container, Fig. 23. Join two containers together, Fig. 24.
5. Thread on a bead, then another container, then a container with legs. Stick these two containers together. Thread on a bead and repeat as before.
6. Thread on the long container, Fig. 25 and stick to the previous one. Thread on the two remaining plastic pieces, plus bead, and join these together with adhesive, except the bead. Make a knot to secure the thread.

Stick on eyes.

Suspend from the nose and the last bead.

This creature makes a delightful noise and should be played around with in order to obtain a variety of movements.

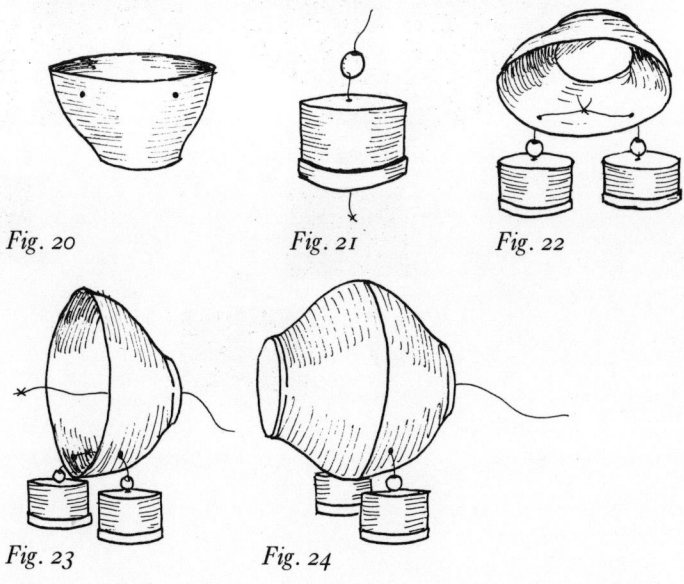

Fig. 20   Fig. 21   Fig. 22

Fig. 23   Fig. 24

21

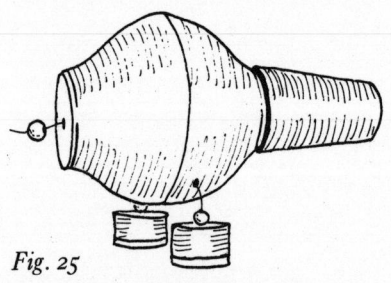

Fig. 25

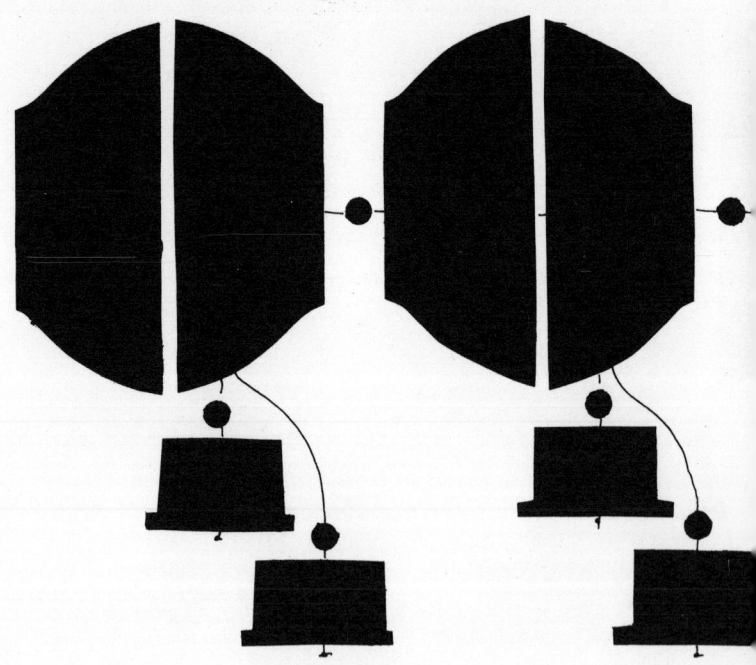

Fig. 26

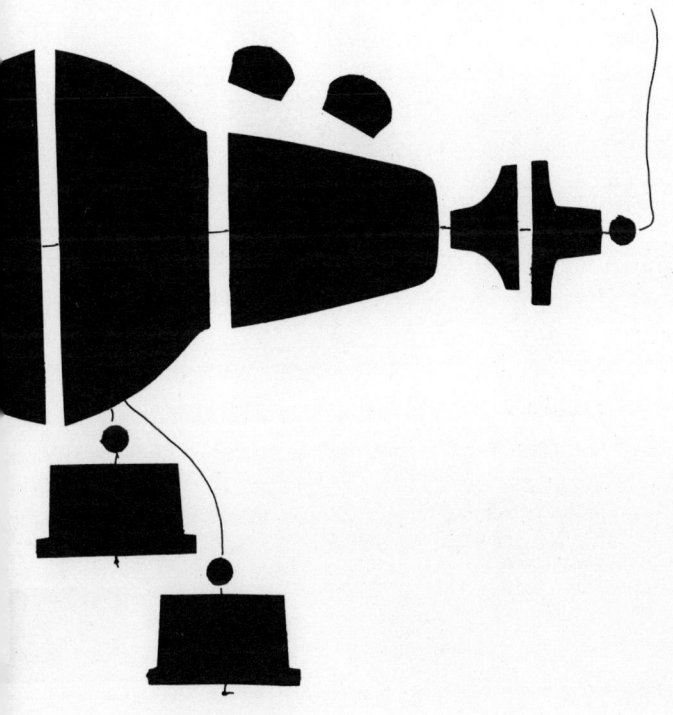

Spy-Lek

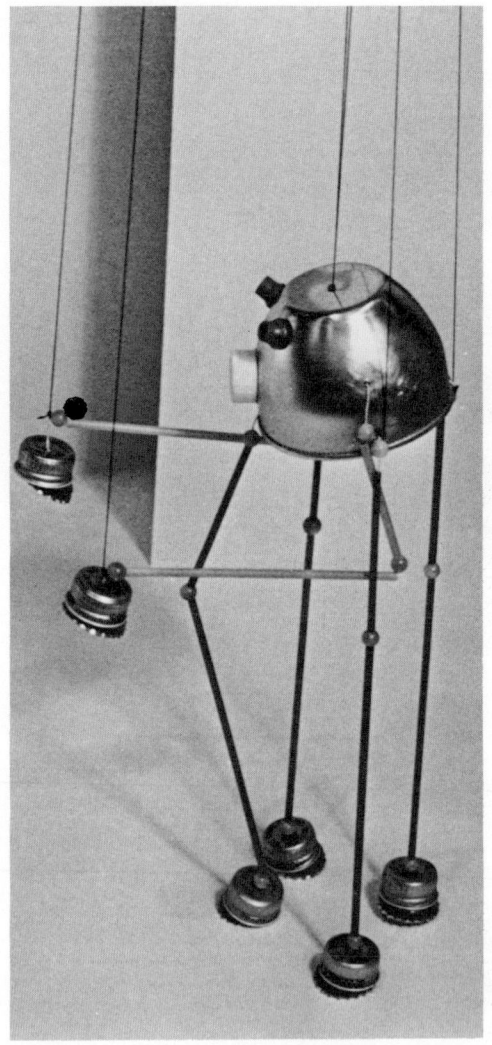

Materials   See Fig. 27. Six lengths of thread 16 in. (40 cm.) long.
required

24

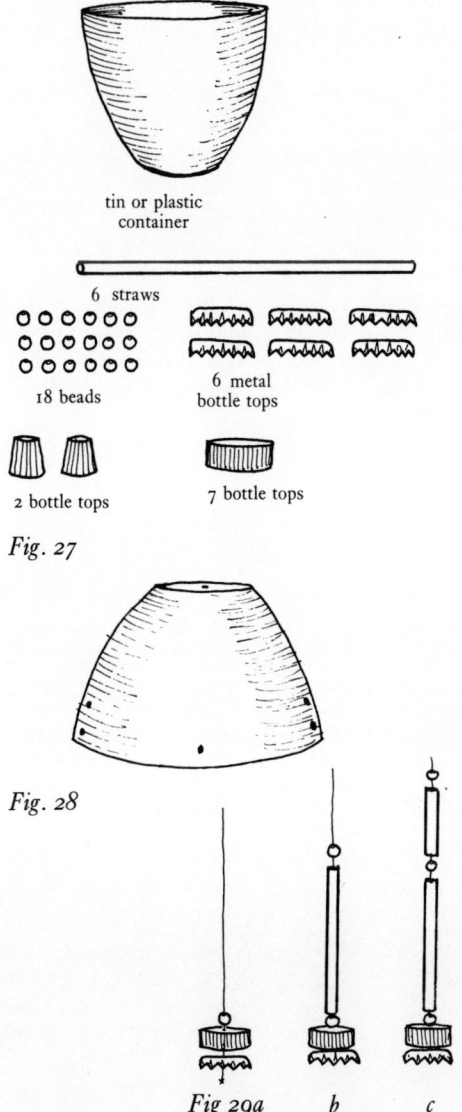

tin or plastic
container

6 straws

18 beads

6 metal
bottle tops

2 bottle tops

7 bottle tops

Fig. 27

Fig. 28

Fig 29a   *b*   *c*

To make   1. Make four holes in the sides of the container to equal the
quarters and near the edge. Put two holes, one at each side, Fig.
28, at a little height up from previous hole.
2. Take length of thread and put a knot on it, and thread on two
different bottle tops and a bead, Fig. 29a.

3. Cut a drinking straw into two, one piece longer than the other. Thread on to leg and put a bead between the straw sections. Finish with a bead, Fig. 29b and c. Make four legs.

4. Thread a leg into the lower hole of the container and secure with a knot and adhesive. Attach all legs.

5. Make two arms like the legs, but a little shorter and attach to the upper holes.

6. Stick on bottle tops for eyes and nose.

To perform Suspend from the top of container, and from the two sides, with one string at the back of the container. These are all attached to a cross bar and hands are attached to the second bar.of the control, Figs. 193 and 194 on page 126.

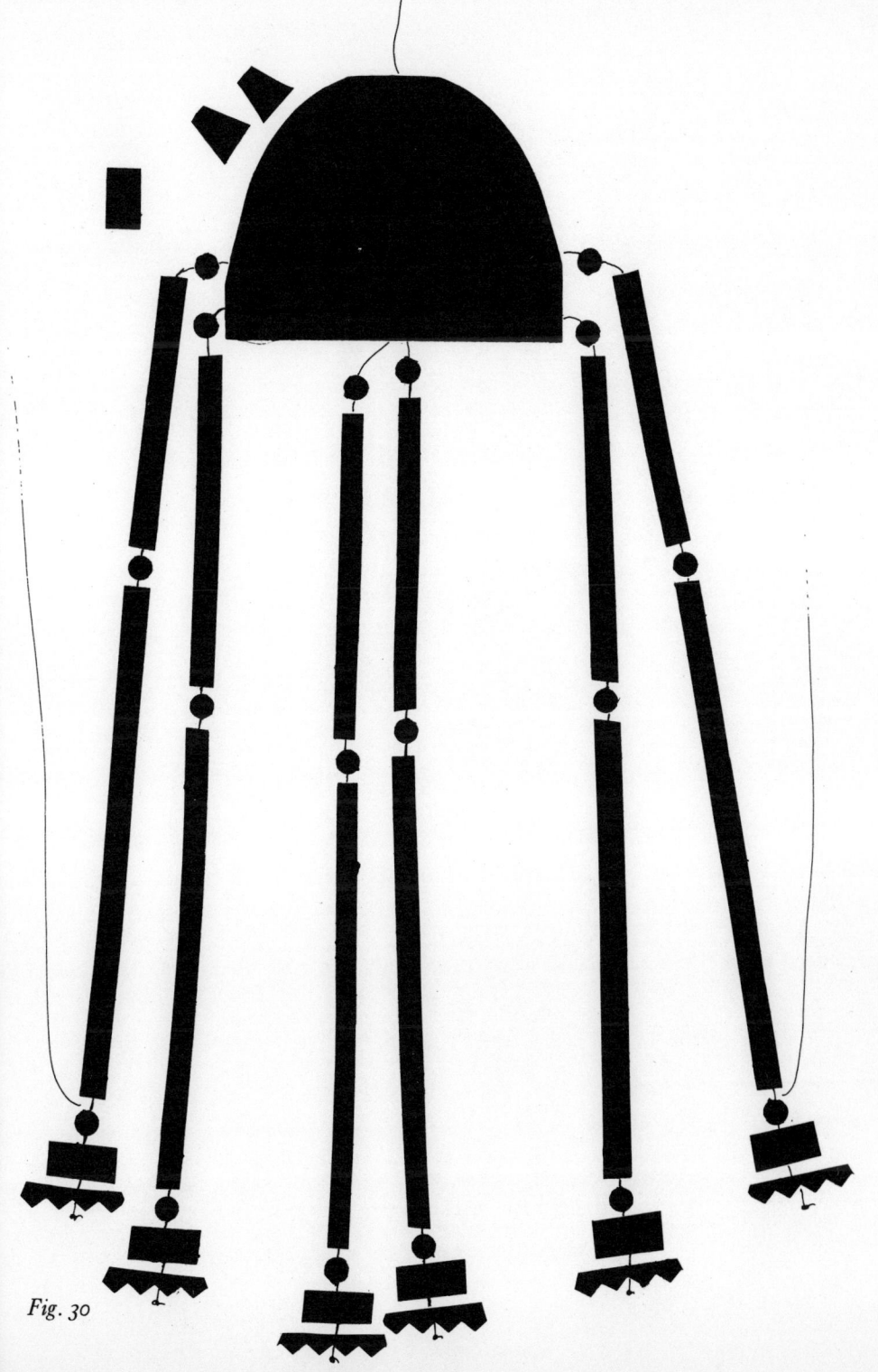

Fig. 30

Ji-Lek

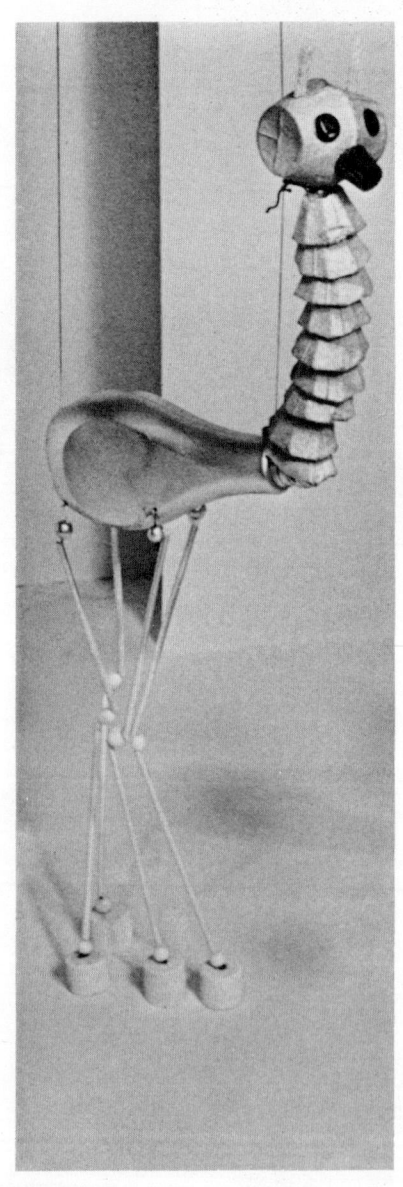

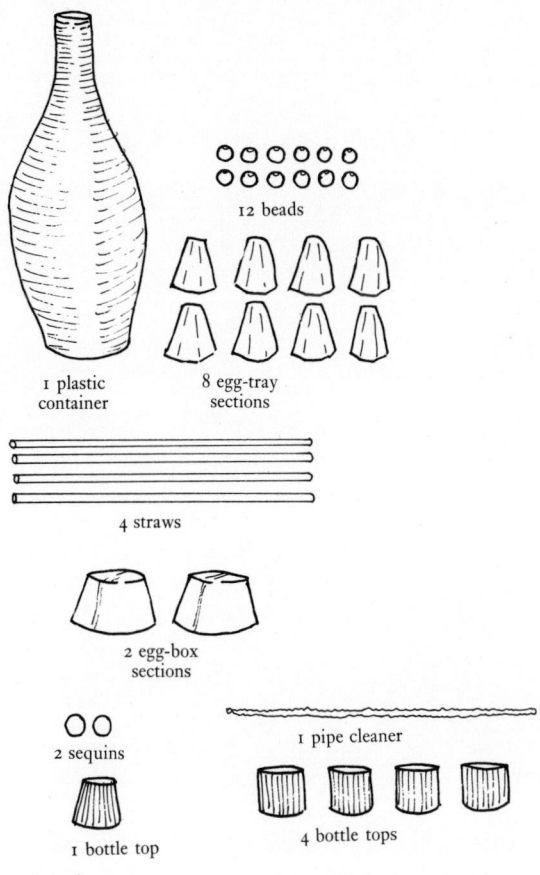

1 plastic
container

12 beads

8 egg-tray
sections

4 straws

2 egg-box
sections

2 sequins

1 pipe cleaner

1 bottle top

4 bottle tops

Fig. 31

Materials required See Fig. 31. Four lengths of thread 14 in. (35 cm.) long. One length 8 in. (20 cm.) expanding curtain wire.

To make
Neck and head

1. Make hole in centre of the small egg-tray sections and thread on to curtain wire, Fig. 32a and b. Let the egg-tray sections overlap and continue for length of neck.

2. Join the two egg-box sections together. Fig. 33.

3. Make a hole in these and insert neck of wire. Secure head in position with adhesive, Fig. 34.

4. Cut pipe-cleaner into two and bend to form ears, and insert into egg-box head, Fig. 35. Stick on bottle top for nose and sequins for eyes, Fig. 36.

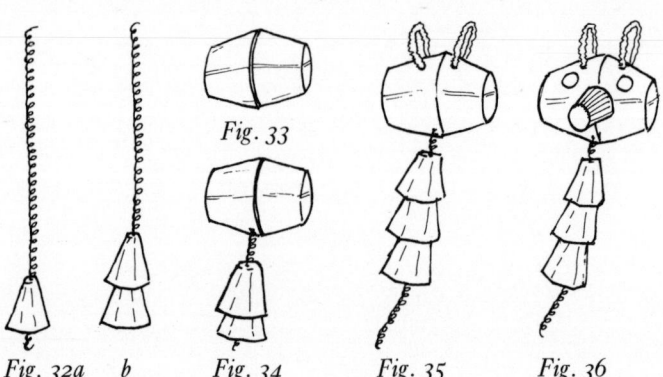

Fig. 33

Fig. 32a   b   Fig. 34   Fig. 35   Fig. 36

Legs

1. Make holes in bottle tops. Then make large knot in thread and thread on a bottle top, a bead, and half a drinking straw, Fig. 37a, b and c.

2. Place a bead between straw sections, ending with a bead, Fig. 37d.

Make four legs like this.

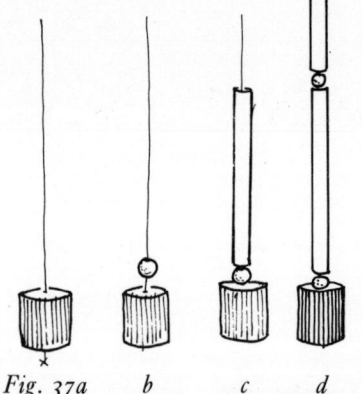

Fig. 37a   b   c   d

Body

1. Make two holes on each side of plastic container for legs and one hole for neck, Fig. 38.

2. Thread a needle with one leg thread and pass through hole made in the body, Fig. 39. Tie on another leg to this thread, Fig. 40. Attach the other two legs in the same way.

3. Push neck wire through the hole at neck end of container and secure with adhesive.

Suspend puppet as in Fig. 193 (page 126) and if the head and neck are too heavy for the body, put aquarium gravel into the container to add weight. Secure all holes so that it does not pour out when the puppet is moved.

30

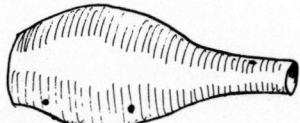

Fig. 38

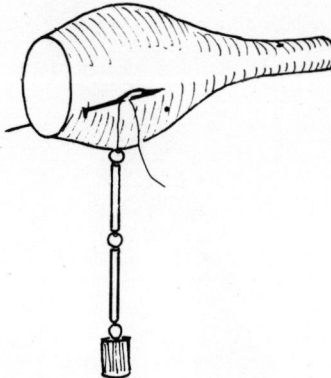

Fig. 39

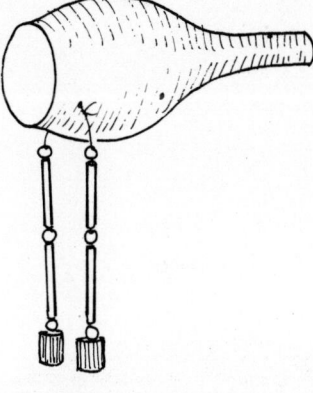

Fig. 40

Fig. 41

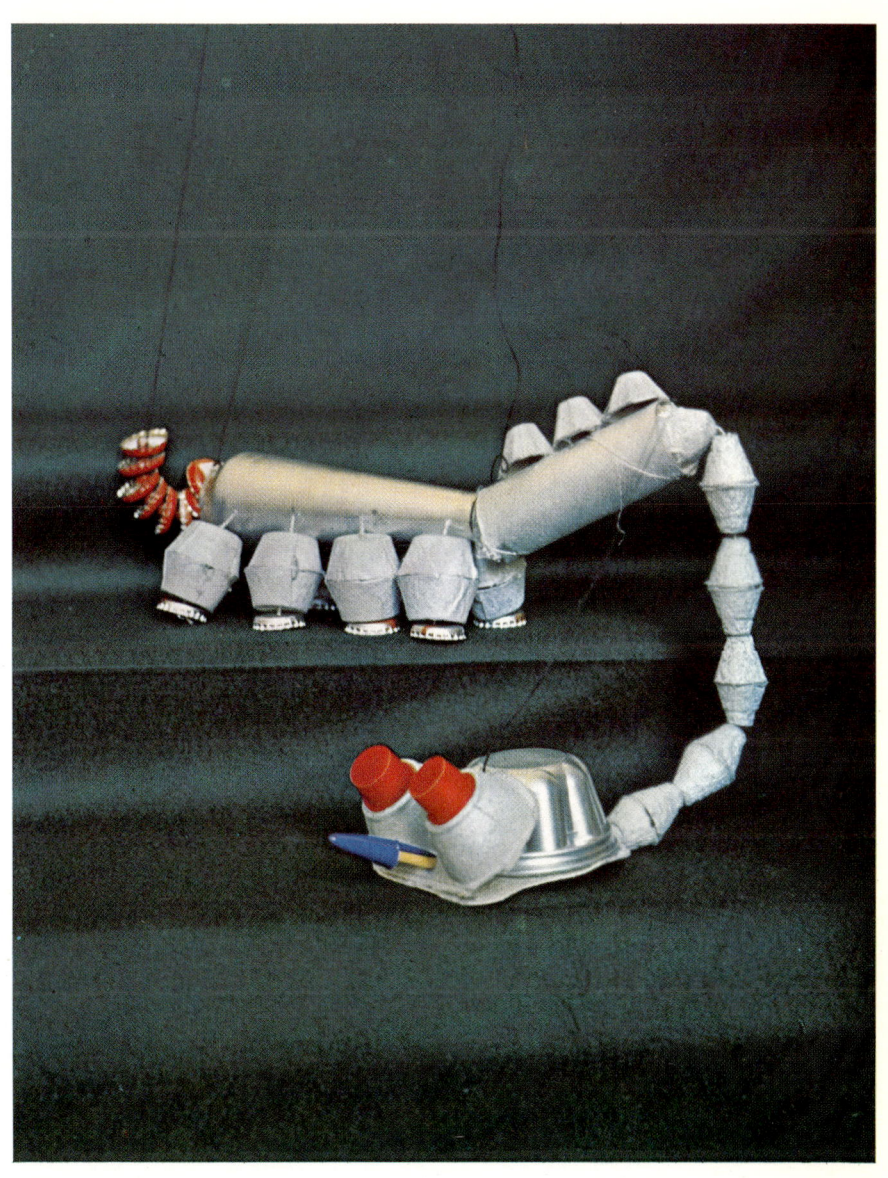

(1) *Verti-Brek (see page 58).*

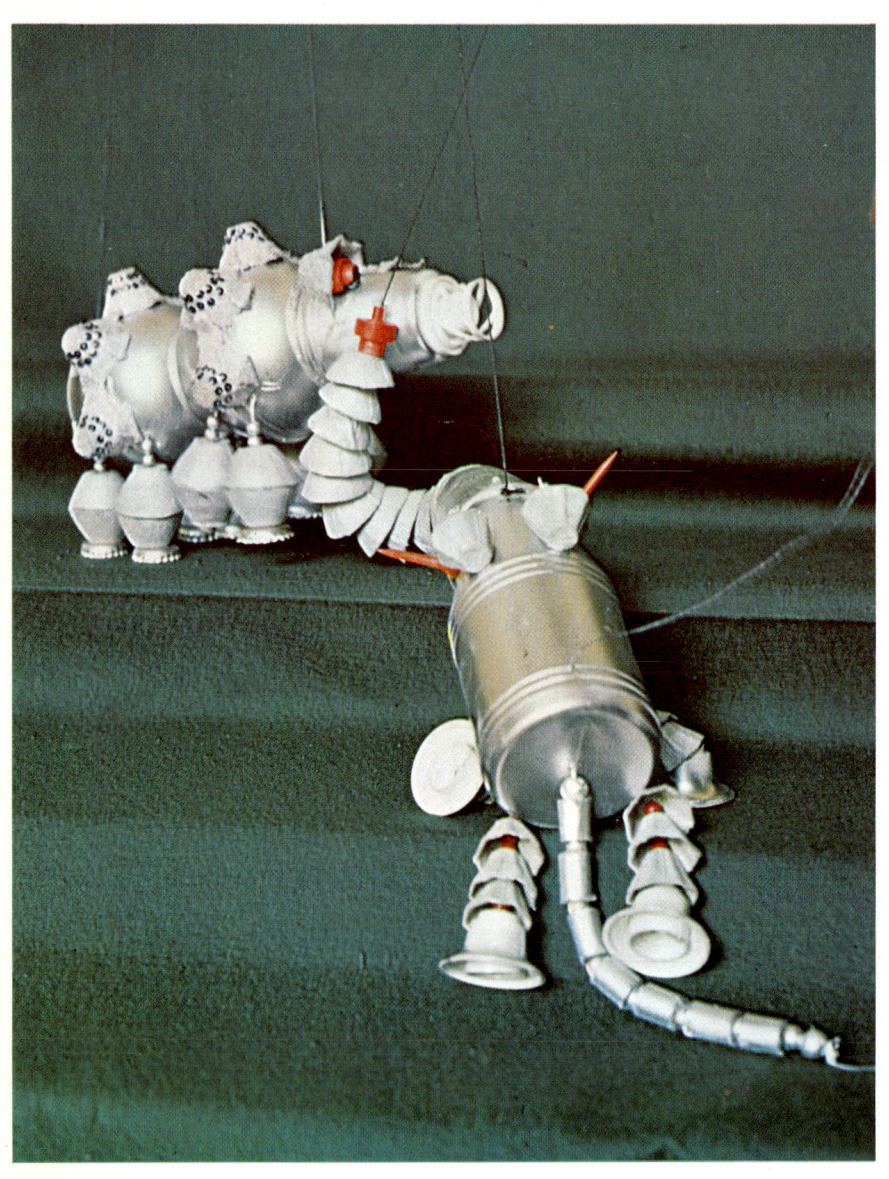

(2) Top: *Luna-Hog*   Bottom: *Ele-Lek* (*see pages 16 and 40*).

Kwok

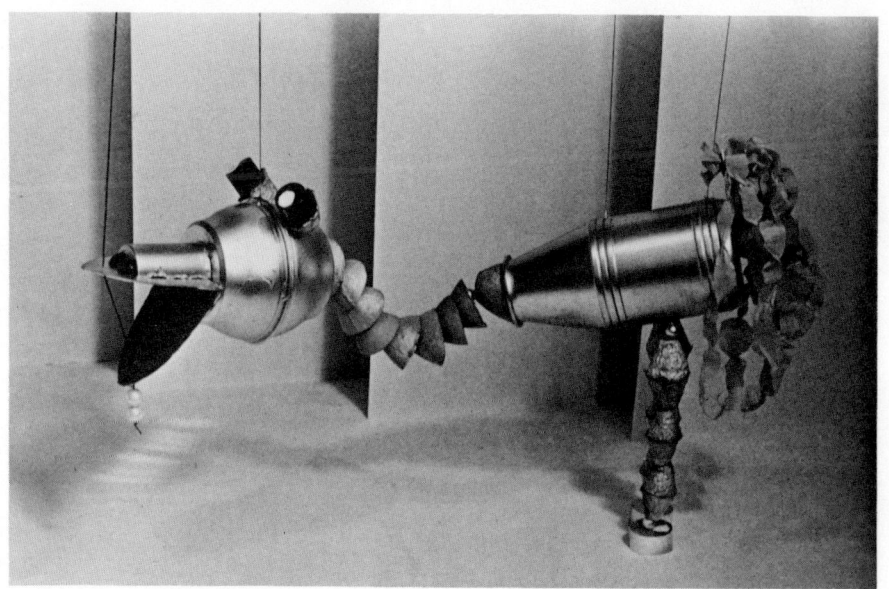

Kwok not only has a long neck which gives great interest in performance, but it also has a mouth which opens and closes.

Materials required
See Fig. 42. Two lengths of thread each 12 in. (30 cm.) long. One length of thread 24 in. (60 cm.) long. Piece of plain cotton 3 by 1 in. (8 by 3 cm.).

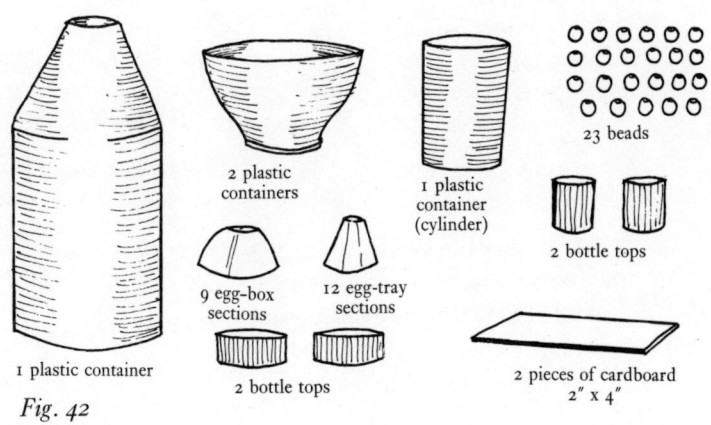

2 plastic containers

1 plastic container (cylinder)

23 beads

2 bottle tops

9 egg-box sections

12 egg-tray sections

1 plastic container

2 bottle tops

2 pieces of cardboard 2″ x 4″

Fig. 42

33

To make

Legs

1. Make a knot in end of thread and thread on bottle top, Fig. 43a.
2. Thread on a bead and an egg-tray section, Fig. 43b.
3. Thread on another egg-tray section and stick to the previous one, Fig. 43c.
4. Thread on four egg-tray sections and stick together in pairs, Fig. 43d. Finally thread on a bead, Fig. 43e.

This completes one leg. Make a second leg in the same way.

5. Attach to body, but first make two holes in the body using a hot needle, Fig. 44. Make a hole in the rear of the container.
6. Thread leg string through the two leg holes and tie second leg to this thread, Figs. 45 and 46.

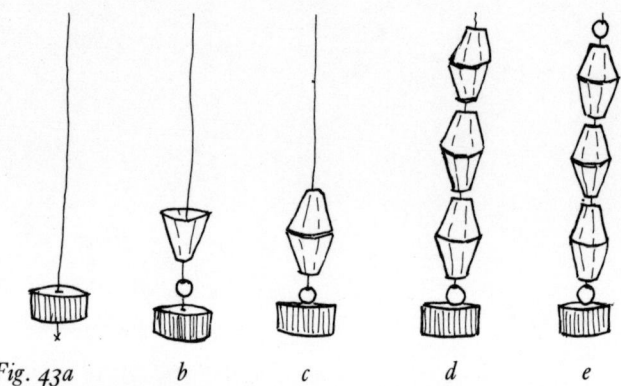

Fig. 43a   *b*   *c*   *d*   *e*

Neck

1. Make two holes in round plastic container, one at base and the other at edge, Fig. 47.
2. Make knot in end of thread and thread through plastic container, Fig. 48.
3. Thread on egg-box section and two beads, Fig. 49.

Continue threading on egg-box sections and two beads alternately, ending with an egg-box section (consult Fig. 60).

4. Pass thread through the long container (use piece of wire with the thread attached by Sellotape for threading). Pull fairly tightly and secure with a bead threaded on to the end of the thread, Fig. 50.
5. Stick neck egg-box section to body.

34

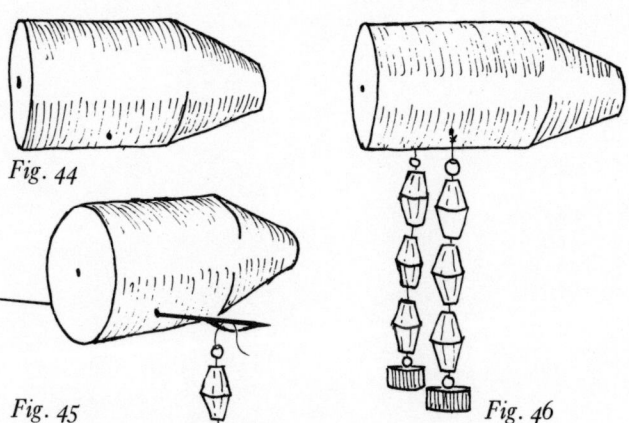

Fig. 44

Fig. 45

Fig. 46

Head

1. To make the mouth, cut two pieces of cardboard to equal the width across the base of the container, and about 1 in. (2·5 cm.) longer than the height of the cylindrical container. Make one end round, Figs. 51 and 52.

2. Attach the lower part of the mouth to base of container, using the strip of fabric. Fold fabric in half (this forms a hinge) and stick one part to the container and one part to the cardboard, Fig. 53.

3. Cut the cylindrical container in half, using a hot needle, Fig. 54a and b.

4. Stick one half to the other piece of cardboard, Fig. 55.

5. Stick this section to head just above previous mouth section, Fig. 56.

6. Before joining the head to neck, pass a thread through the container of neck (this is the performing thread, Fig. 57) then stick the two sections together, Fig. 58.

7. Pass a thread through both parts of mouth for performing, and also attach two beads to a short piece of thread and fasten to lower mouth (this will give weight to allow the mouth to open easily, Fig. 59).

8. To finish off, stick on bottle tops for eyes and beads or buttons for nostrils. The lower mouth may be coloured red.

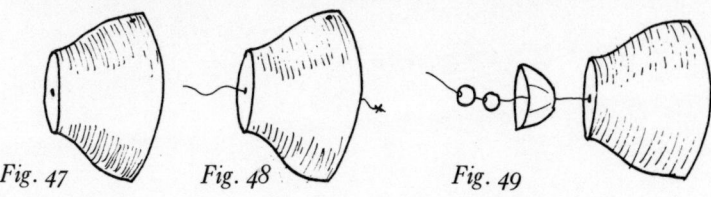

Fig. 47

Fig. 48

Fig. 49

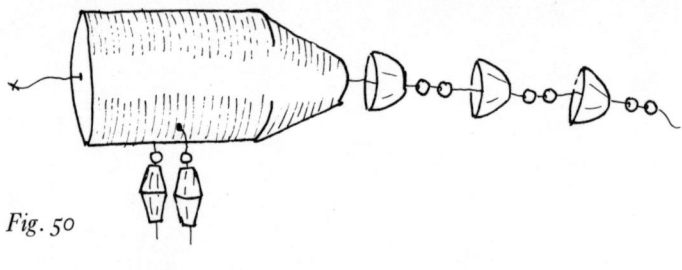

Fig. 50

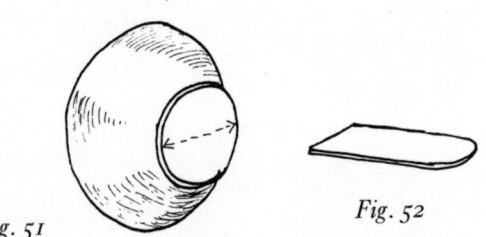

Fig. 51

Fig. 52

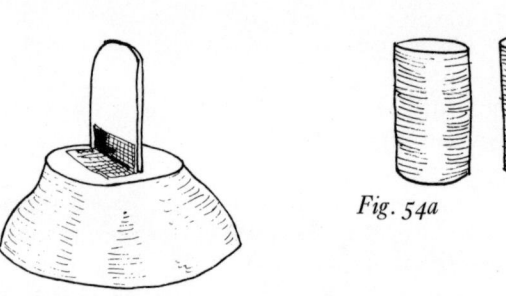

Fig. 53

Fig. 54a   *b*

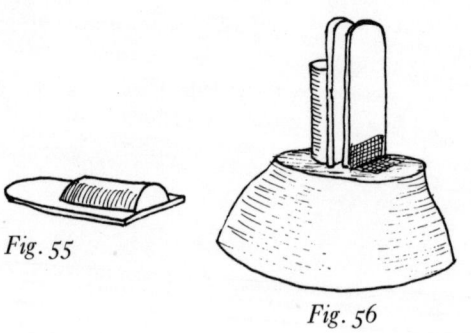

Fig. 55

Fig. 56

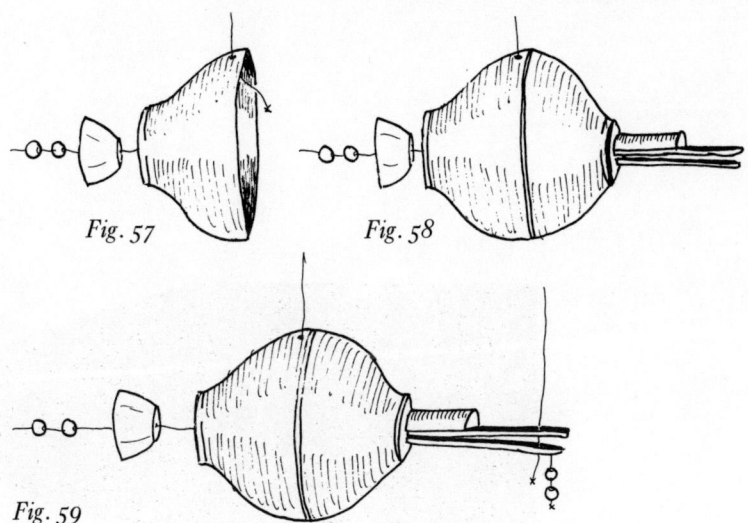

Fig. 57

Fig. 58

Fig. 59

To perform Suspend the body on a separate thread from the head (see page 124).

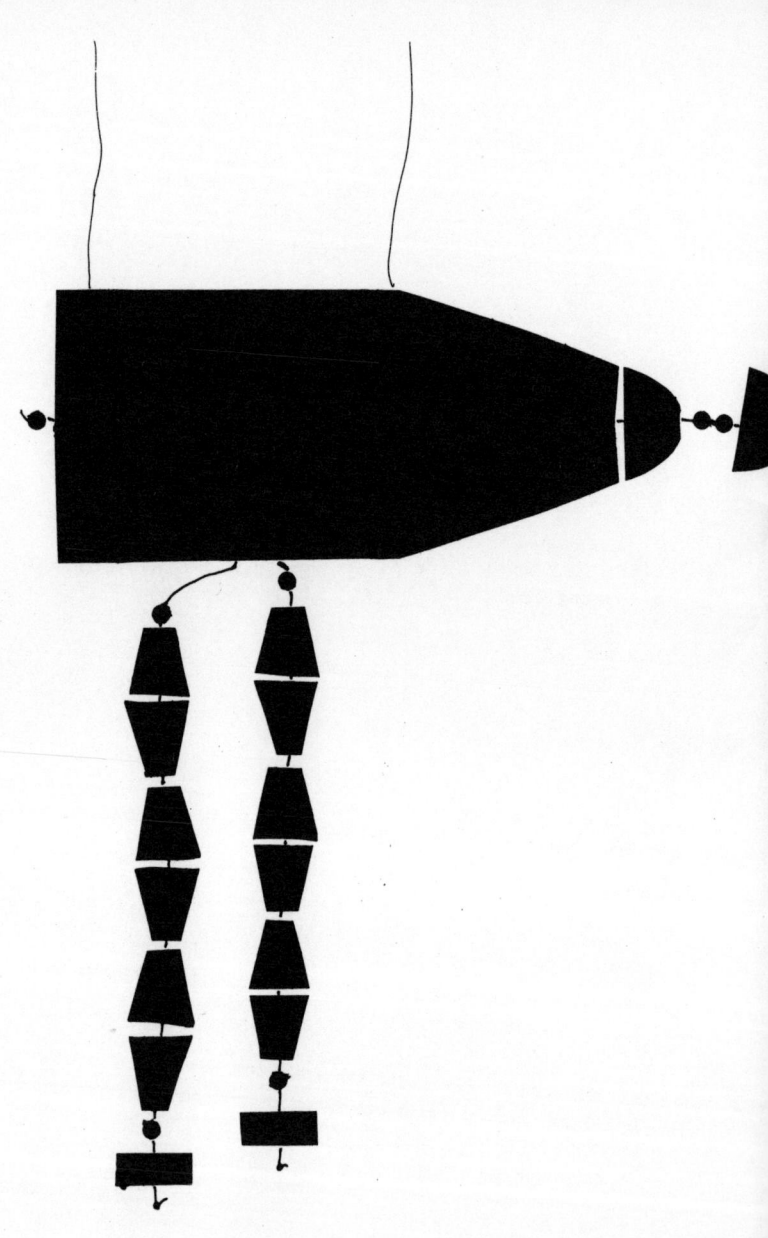

Fig. 60

Ele-Lek

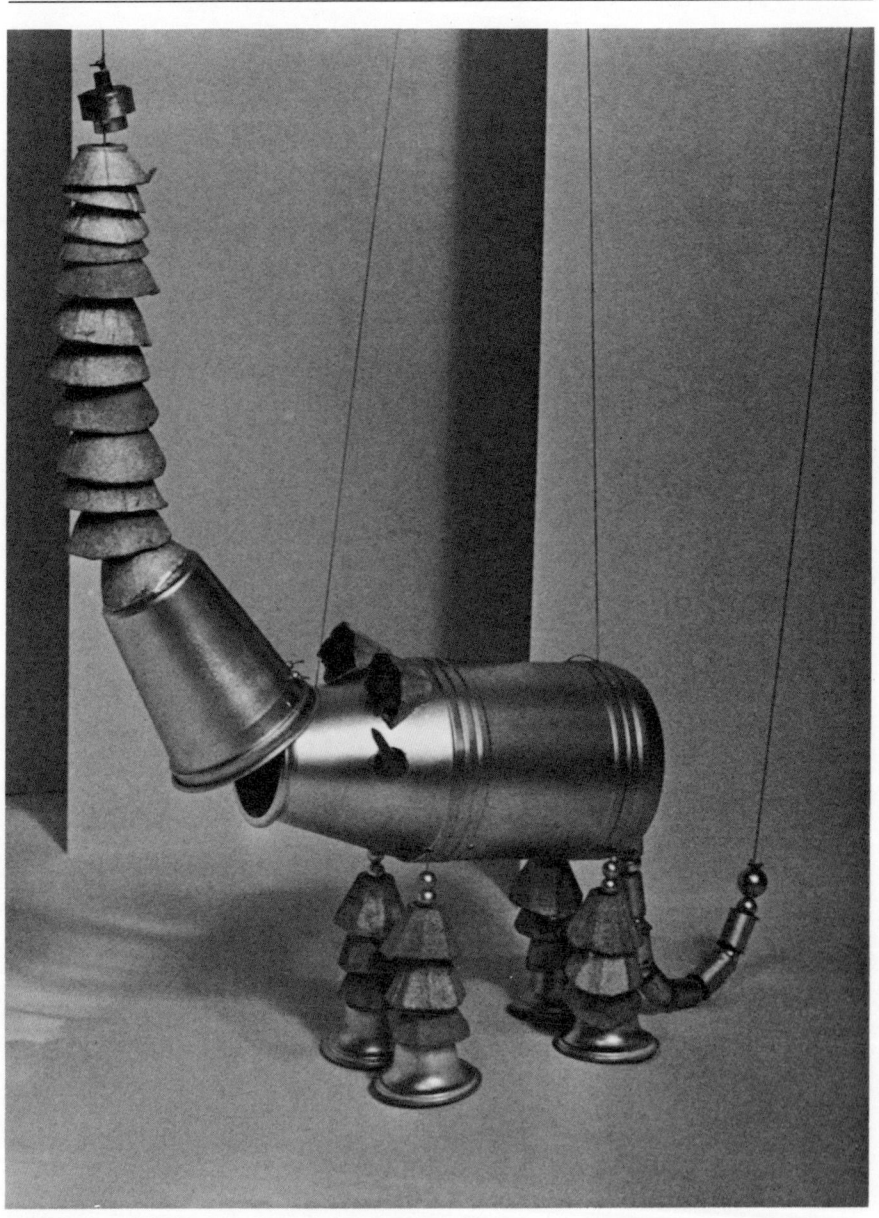

<table>
<tr><td>Materials
required</td><td>See Fig. 61. Four lengths of thread 12 in. (30 cm.) long. One length of thread 18 in. (45 cm.) long. One length of thread 15 in. (38 cm.) long.</td></tr>
</table>

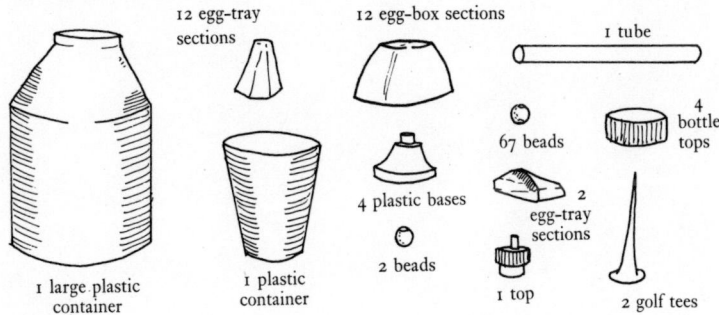

12 egg-tray sections

12 egg-box sections

1 tube

67 beads

4 bottle tops

4 plastic bases

2 egg-tray sections

2 beads

1 top

2 golf tees

1 large plastic container

1 plastic container

Fig. 61

To make

Legs

1. Put a good sized knot on the end of the 12-in. thread and thread on a bottle top, Fig. 62a. Then add two beads, Fig. 62b.
2. Thread on a plastic base and two beads, Fig. 62c.
3. Thread on an egg-tray section and two beads, Fig. 62d.
4. Add another egg-tray section and two beads, Fig. 62e.
5. Add another egg-tray section and one bead, Fig. 62f. This completes one leg.

Make four legs.

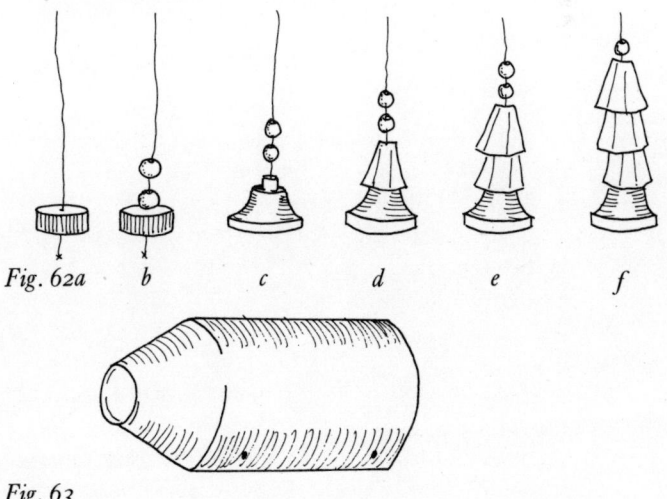

Fig. 62a   *b*   *c*   *d*   *e*   *f*

Fig. 63

41

Fig. 64

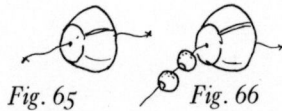

Fig. 65   *Fig. 66*

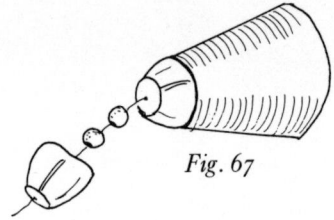

Fig. 67

Body

1. Make four holes for the legs by pushing a hot needle through the large plastic container, Fig. 63.
2. Make a hole in the base of the container for the tail thread.
3. Thread a needle with a leg thread, and pass through the holes in the container, Fig. 64. Tie on the other leg to the thread, secure and knot, Fig. 64.

Attach the other leg.

Snout

1. Take the 18-in. long length of thread and knot the end, and thread on an egg-box section, Fig. 65.
2. Thread on two beads and another egg-box section, Fig. 66. Repeat this until twelve egg-box sections are on, and finish with

42

a Squezy bottle top. Put knot in thread to hold all secure.

3. Stick the snout on to the small plastic container, Fig. 67.

4. Attach container to larger one with a piece of thread to form a hinge, Fig. 68.

Tail   Pass a thread through the end of the container and put a large knot on the end to prevent it pulling through. Cut the tube into eight pieces and thread a bead and a piece of tube alternately on to the tail thread, ending with two beads. Secure with a knot, Fig. 68.

Attach egg-tray sections for eyes, then spray with paint. Stick on bright beads for eyes and two golf tees.

Fig. 68

Luna-Mog

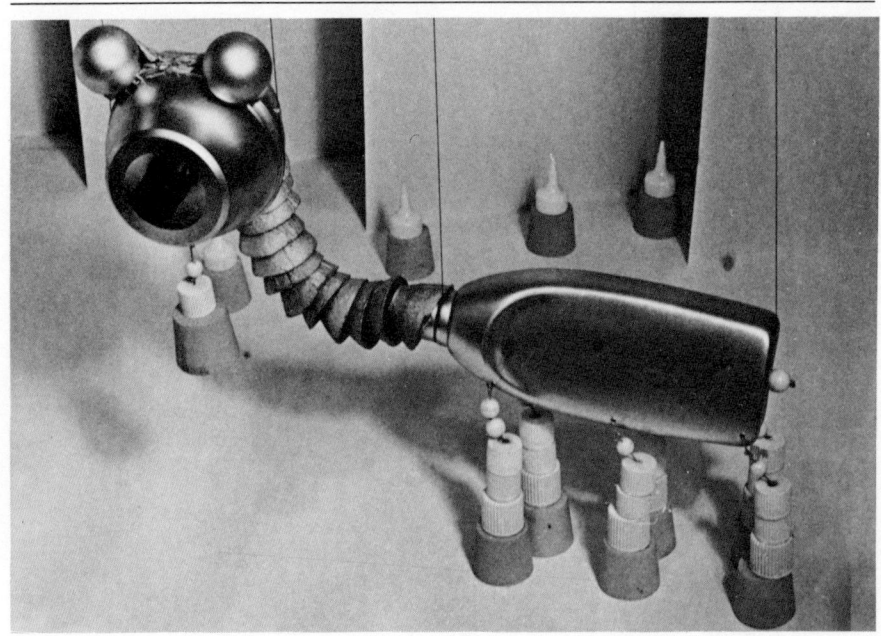

Materials required See Fig. 69. Six lengths of thread each 12 in. (30 cm.) long. One length of thread 30 in. (75 cm.) long. One length of thread 6 in. (15 cm.) long.

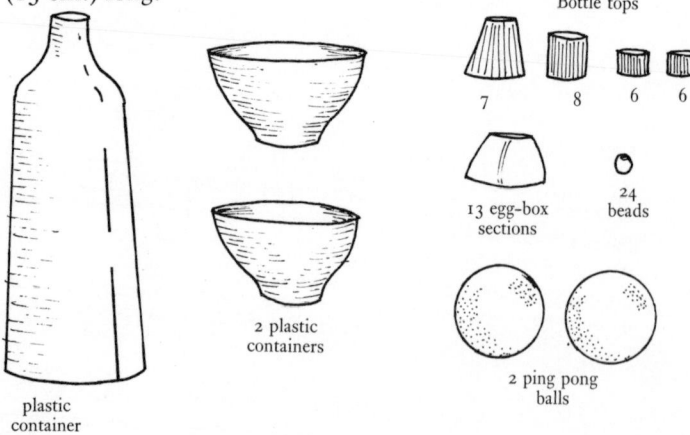

plastic container

Fig. 69

2 plastic containers

Bottle tops

7   8   6   6

13 egg-box sections

24 beads

2 ping pong balls

46

Preparation Make holes in all the bottle tops.

To make

Legs
1. Make a large knot in end of 12-in. thread and thread on a large bottle top, Fig. 70a.
2. Thread on the next size of bottle top, Fig. 70b.
3. Thread on the next two sizes of bottle top, Fig. 70c. The bottle tops should all be stuck together to form a solid leg. Finish off with a knot.
4. Thread a bead and make a knot, Fig. 70d.
5. Make six legs, putting two beads at the top of two of the legs, Fig. 73.

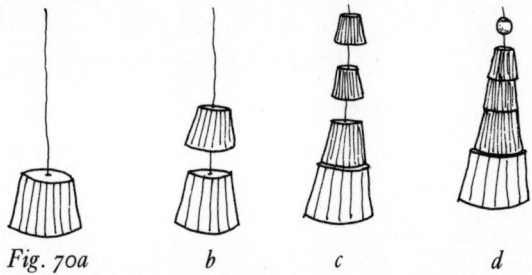

Fig. 70a   *b*   *c*   *d*

Body
1. Make six holes in the lower part of the plastic container (three on each side) Fig. 71.
2. Pass the leg thread through the eye of a needle and pass the needle through the container, and tie two leg threads together as in Fig. 72.

Put on the next pair of legs and then attach the two legs which have the two beads at the top, as in Fig. 73.

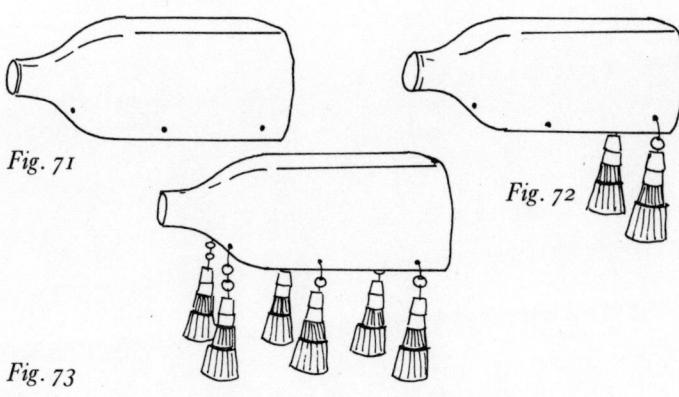

Fig. 71

Fig. 72

Fig. 73

47

Head   1. Make a knot in end of 6-in. thread and thread on a large bottle top, then the smaller one. Stick together, Fig. 74.
2. Make knot in thread and thread on bead, then make a knot, Fig. 75.
3. Thread on to plastic bowl, Fig. 76 and secure end of thread with a knot inside the container.
4. Make a knot on the end of long length of thread and add a large bead. Pass the thread through the two plastic bowls, Fig. 77, and stick them together.
5. Dip a piece of wadding into a paste and mould it into position, using the two ping-pong balls as eyes, Fig. 78. Leave for a day or two to dry thoroughly.

This section will not stick to the plastic, but will dry with a moulded shape. It is then attached to the containers with adhesive.

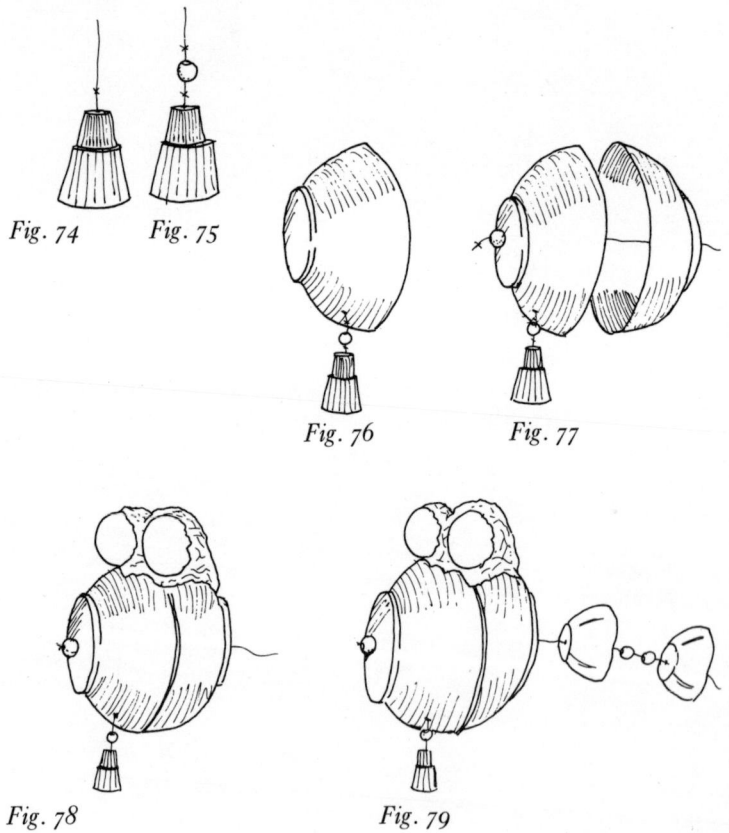

Fig. 74   Fig. 75

Fig. 76   Fig. 77

Fig. 78   Fig. 79

(*3*) *Luna-Mog (see page 46).*

(4)   *Earth People (see page 109).*

Neck   Thread on a bead and an egg-box section alternately. Pass the end of thread through the container (body) and pull the end of the thread fairly tight. Thread on a bead, make a secure knot, and put on a spot of adhesive to secure.

To finish stick bottle top over bead for nose.

To perform Suspend the body from a stick, putting the head on to a separate one.

Note   The head and body may be sprayed with paint, but keep the legs and bottle tops under the chin their original colour by wrapping them with paper before spraying.

Fig. 80

Moggies

These are little creatures belonging to the Luna-Mog family. When an army is required, a number of these can be made quite quickly.

Each Moggie is made from a bottle top the same size and shape as used for Luna-Mog with a slender pointed top added. These two tops are threaded on to a long length of thread and then stuck together. All the Moggies are attached to one control so that they all move together. Any number can be attached, but difficulties may arise by the threads becoming tangled.

To store, simply wind the threads on to the control.

Armies can be made from other groups of bottle tops. If they are too light when suspended, fill with Plasticine, which should enable the tops to hang down straight.

Performance: these types of toys may be suspended to form shapes or patterns in performance, like small dancers, or a chorus.

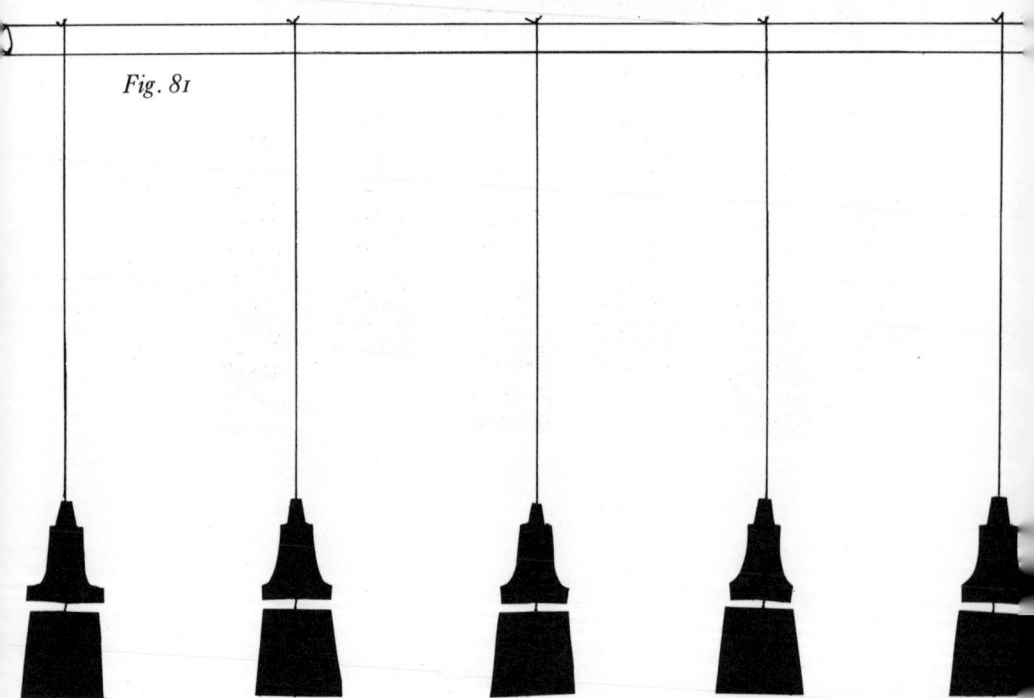

Fig. 81

Shag-a-Lek

This puppet has a much longer neck and larger head than previous creatures. The scale of this puppet is such that when performed with the earth people, they look very small. The creature can make a noise with its feet, but the greatest interest is in the length of its neck and the mobility of the head. It has two eyes in the front of its head and two at the back, so that to such expressions as "You cannot have seen so-and-so because you haven't got eyes at the back of your head," Shag-a-Lek can reply, "Of course I saw them with my very eyes, you forget I have eyes at the back of my head."

Materials required

See Fig. 82. One piece of wire $6\frac{1}{2}$ in. (16 cm.) long. One piece of wire 8 in. (20 cm.) long. One piece of wire 10 in. (25 cm.) long. One length of thread 36 in. (90 cm.) long. Six lengths of thread each 6 in. (15 cm.) long. One skein brightly-coloured thick nylon yarn. Two nylon net fruit containers.

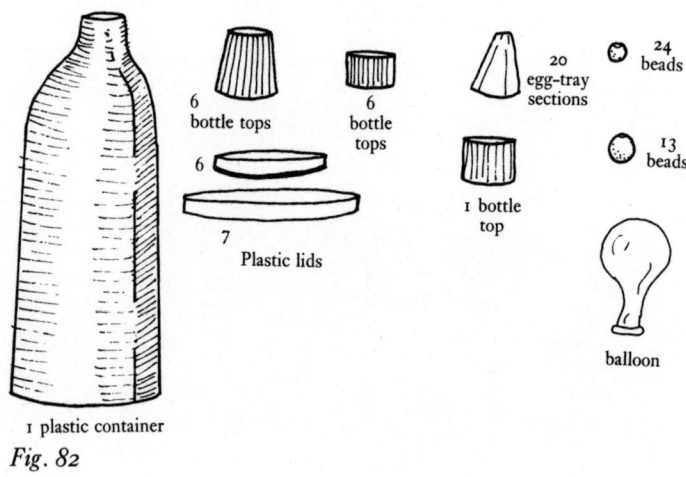

6 bottle tops

6 bottle tops

6

7 Plastic lids

20 egg-tray sections

24 beads

13 beads

1 bottle top

balloon

1 plastic container

Fig. 82

To make

Body

1. Make six holes in the plastic container using a hot needle. Push the needle right through the container each time, then push the wire through, the shortest piece at the front, Fig. 83. Make two holes in rear for suspending, Fig. 84. Bend ends of wire round to form loops, or cover well with Sellotape.
2. Using a short piece of thread, make a knot and thread on a large bottle top, then a smaller one, Fig. 85.
3. Thread on four beads, Fig. 86. This forms one leg. Make six legs the same.
4. Attach the legs to the ends of the wires, Fig. 87.

The body can now be covered with lengths of nylon yarn. Stick this to the top of the body but leave ends hanging down at the sides.

The rear of the body can easily be covered by cutting nylon yarn into small pieces, then sprinkling the small pieces on the rear with adhesive.

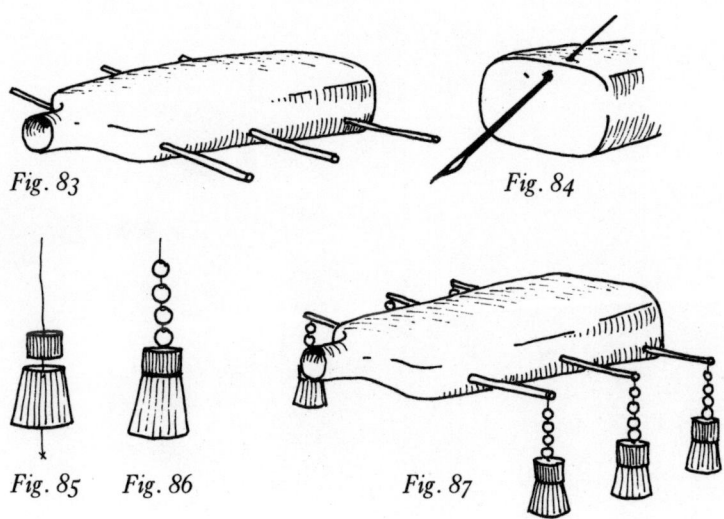

Fig. 83

Fig. 84

Fig. 85   Fig. 86

Fig. 87

Head and Neck

1. Blow up a balloon and cover it with six or seven layers of paper, pasting one layer on top of the previous one. Leave to dry. Cover with net and stick.

2. Make a knot on the long length of thread and pass through the bottle top, Fig. 89. Follow this chart, threading on the various sizes of plastic lids alternately, with the egg-tray sections and beads.

3. Secure the end of thread by stitching into the net on the balloon. Attach the other end of neck A to A of the body and stick securely together.

Note

Colour may be added to the egg-tray sections by sticking on the coloured nylon yarn. Strands of the yarn may also be threaded into the net and the ends left loose, to form a beard.

Features should be added and anything else to give character.

The head is suspended by threading a length of thread down through the balloon at the front, and a length should be partly threaded through the balloon from one side to the other. These three threads are used for suspending the head and to give balance.

Balloons are not easy to suspend and balance plays a very important part.

55

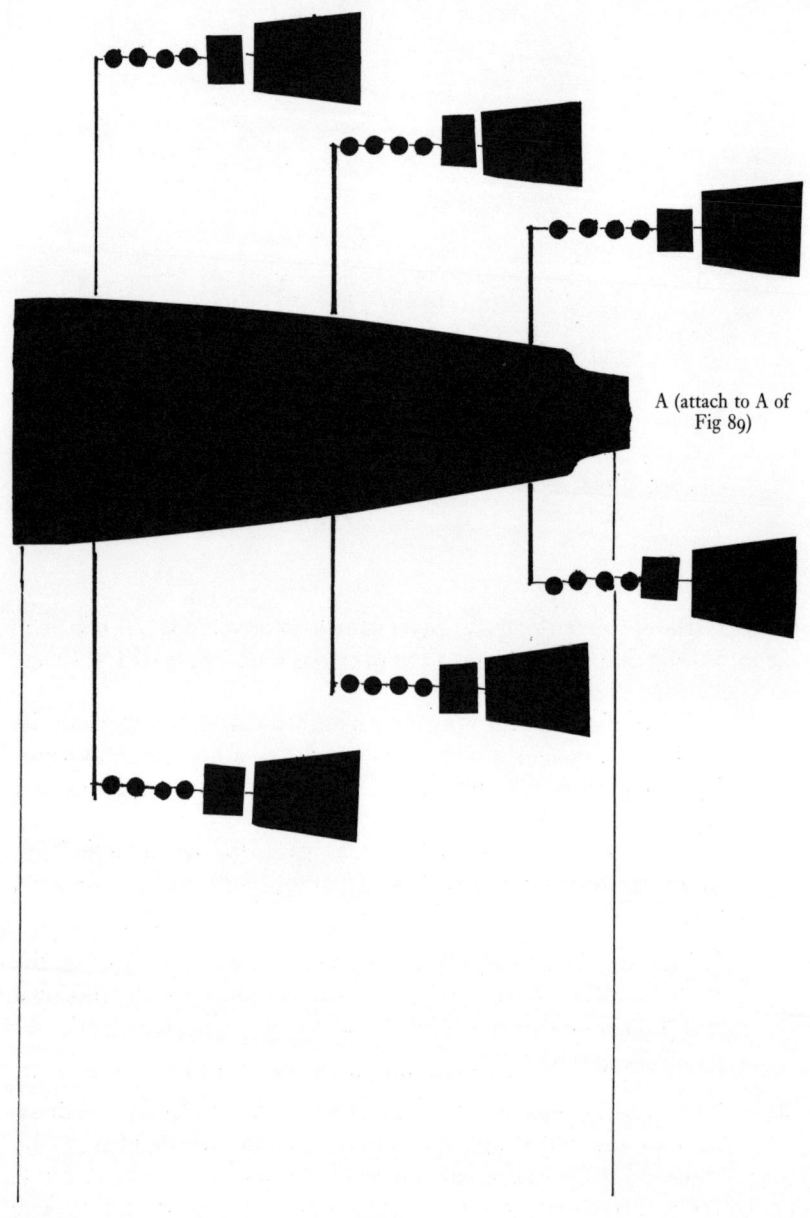

A (attach to A of Fig 89)

Fig. 88

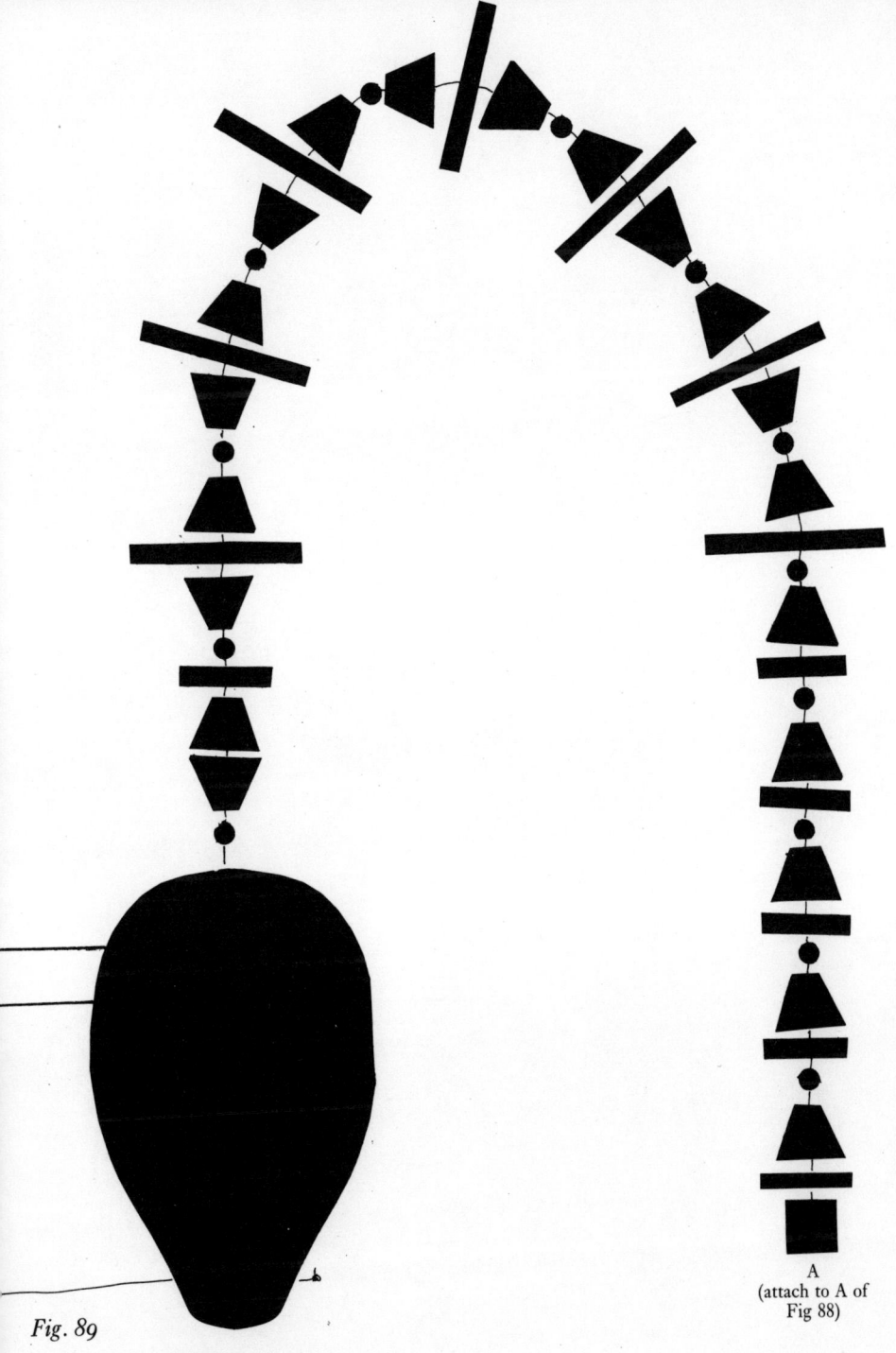

Fig. 89

A
(attach to A of
Fig 88)

Verti-Brek

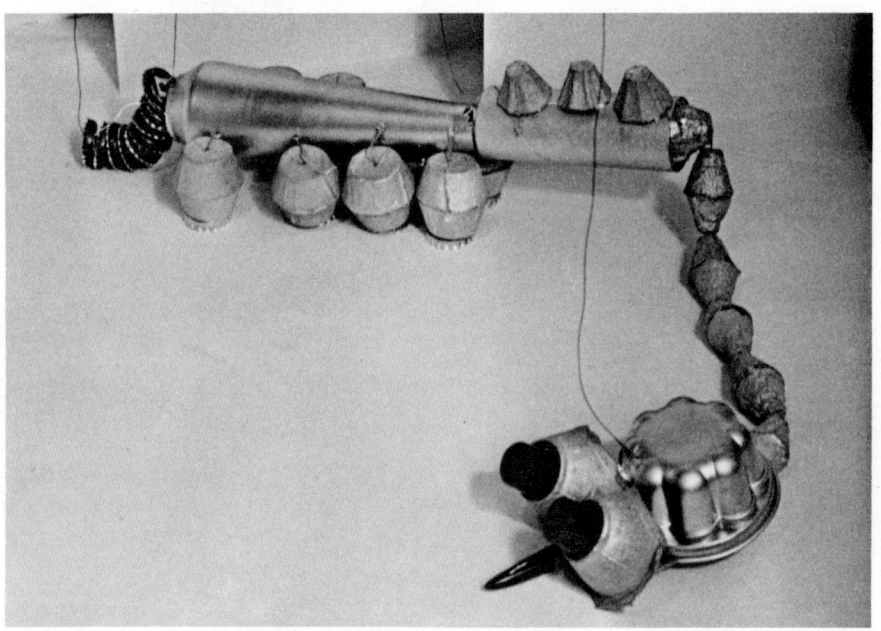

Materials required See Fig. 90. Nine lengths of thread each 12 in. (30 cm.) long. One length of thread 30 in. (76 cm.) long.

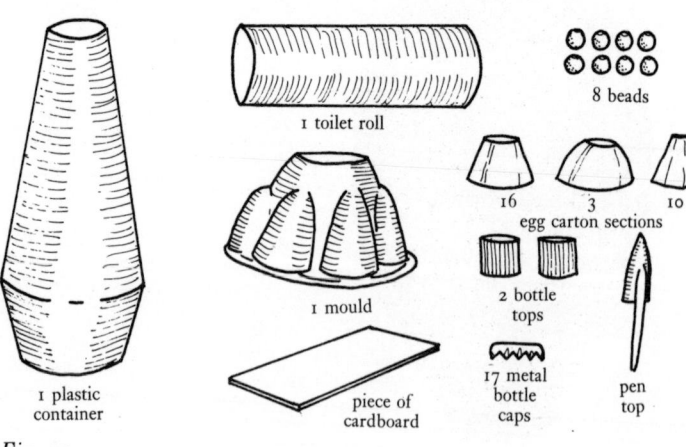

8 beads

1 toilet roll

16   3   10
egg carton sections

2 bottle tops

1 mould

17 metal bottle caps

pen top

1 plastic container

piece of cardboard

Fig. 90

58

To make   1. Make a large knot in end of shorter length of thread and thread on one bottle cap and two egg-tray sections, Fig. 91a. Stick the cartons together. Make eight legs the same way.

2. Using a hot needle make eight holes in the container for the legs. To do this, push the needle right through the container for each pair of legs, Fig. 91b.

3. Thread a needle with a leg thread and pass through two holes in the body, Fig. 92. Tie a second leg to this thread. Attach all legs in this way.

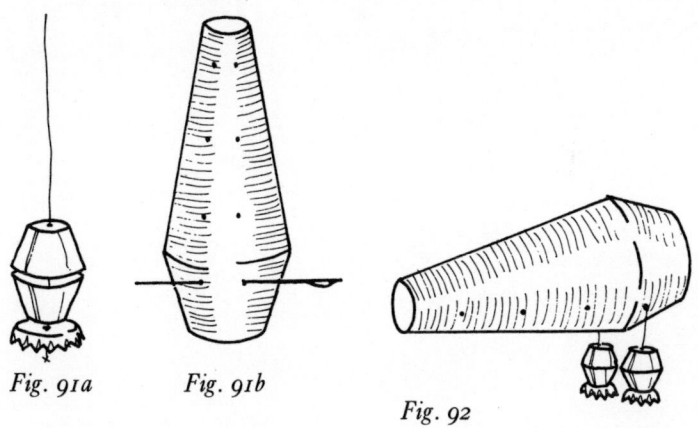

Fig. 91a   Fig. 91b

Fig. 92

Neck and   1. Make a knot in the end of thread and pass through the one
head   rounded egg-box section, Fig. 93.

2. Stick this to end of toilet roll tube, Fig. 94.

3. Thread on all the egg-tray sections and stick in pairs, Fig. 95.

4. Place plastic mould on to cardboard and draw round. Cut away the back part of the cardboard, Fig. 96a and b. The extended end (front) should be about half the length of another mould.

5. Pass the neck thread up through the back part of the cardboard, Fig. 97, and up through the mould, Fig. 98. Make a knot in thread. Stick the mould to the cardboard, completely hiding the rear of the cardboard.

6. Stick on the twin egg-carton sections for eyes and also the bottle tops, Fig. 99. Push in a pen top for nose.

7. Stick neck to plastic container at an angle.

59

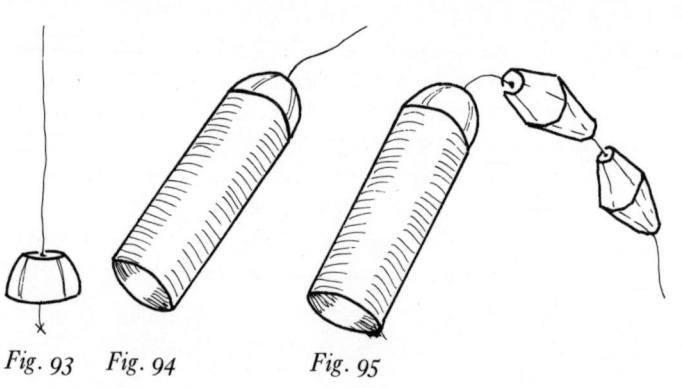

Fig. 93   *Fig. 94*   *Fig. 95*

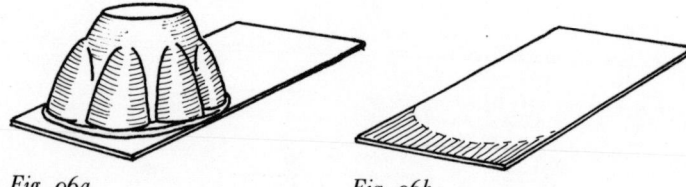

Fig. 96a   *Fig. 96b*

Fig. 97   *Fig. 98*

Fig. 99

| *Tail* | The tail is made by threading bottle caps and beads alternately on to the length of thread, Fig. 100. Make two holes in the rear of the animal, Fig. 101, and thread the tail through these holes and secure by tying. |

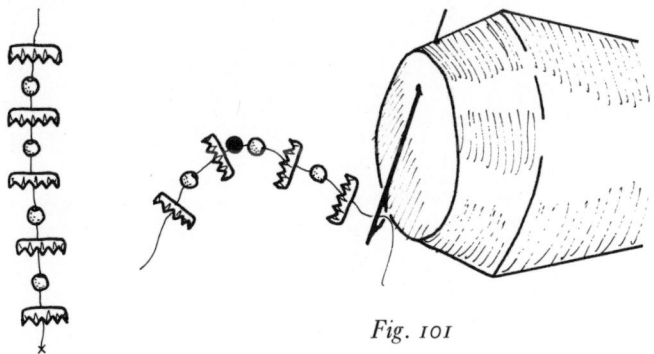

Fig. 100   Fig. 101

To perform Suspend the body from the rear and front end on a single control and hold the head by a single thread from the front of the mould. This will enable the head to perform independently of the body and movement should be experimented with to obtain a wide variety of interest.

Left : Verti-Brek   Background : Moggies   Right : Luna-Mog

Fig. 102

Go-Lek

This delightful character is best made from colourful throw-away materials. The plastic lids used for the neck and head and the bottle-tops for the feet were the same colour. Metal bottle caps of the same colour were stuck on to parts of the egg-tray pinnacles on the body.

Materials required

See Fig. 103. Six pieces of thread each 12 in. (30 cm.) long. One piece of thread 36 in. (90 cm.) long. Three pieces of thread each 20 in. (51 cm.) long. A piece of egg-tray with tops removed from pinnacles to form holes.

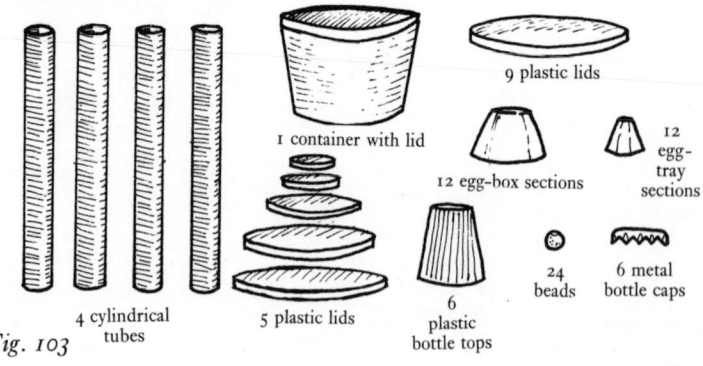

9 plastic lids

1 container with lid

12 egg-box sections

12 egg-tray sections

4 cylindrical tubes

5 plastic lids

6 plastic bottle tops

24 beads

6 metal bottle caps

Fig. 103

64

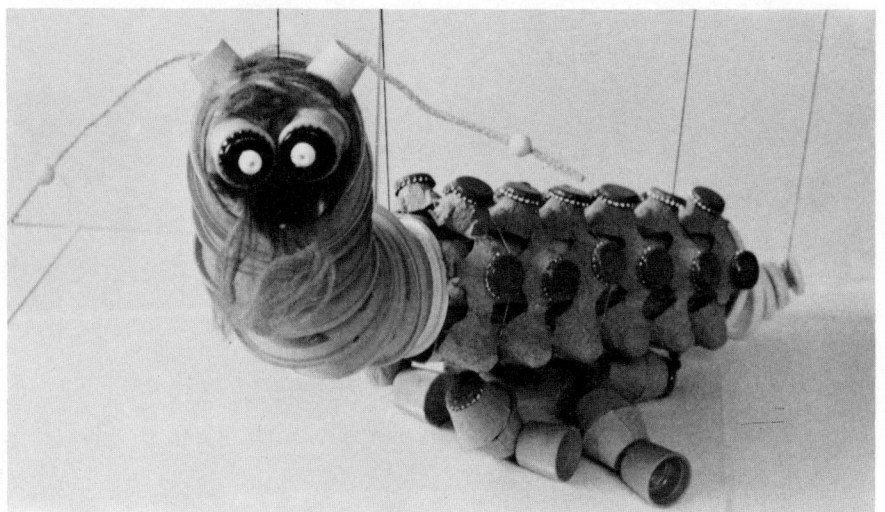

To make

Legs   1. Make a knot in end of thread and thread on plastic bottle top, Fig. 104a. Make another knot. (Beads may be used in place of knots.)
2. Thread on a pair of egg-box sections and stick together, Fig. 104b. Then add a bottle cap.

Make six legs in this way.

Body   1. Place the four cylinders together and bind with adhesive tape, Fig. 104c.
2. Wrap egg-tray sections around body and tie in three places, Fig. 104d. Adhesive may also be used to keep it secure.
3. Attach the legs to the body by tying the leg threads to the body threads, Fig. 104e. Stick in place with adhesive.

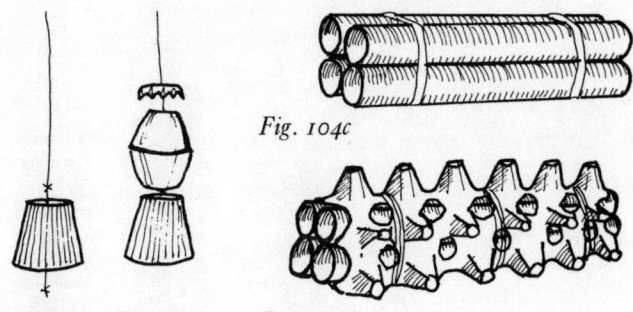

Fig. 104c

Fig. 104a   Fig. 104b   Fig. 104d

Fig. 104e

Tail and neck   1. Put knot in the end of the thread and thread on the plastic lids and egg-tray sections, grading up the size as in Fig. 105.

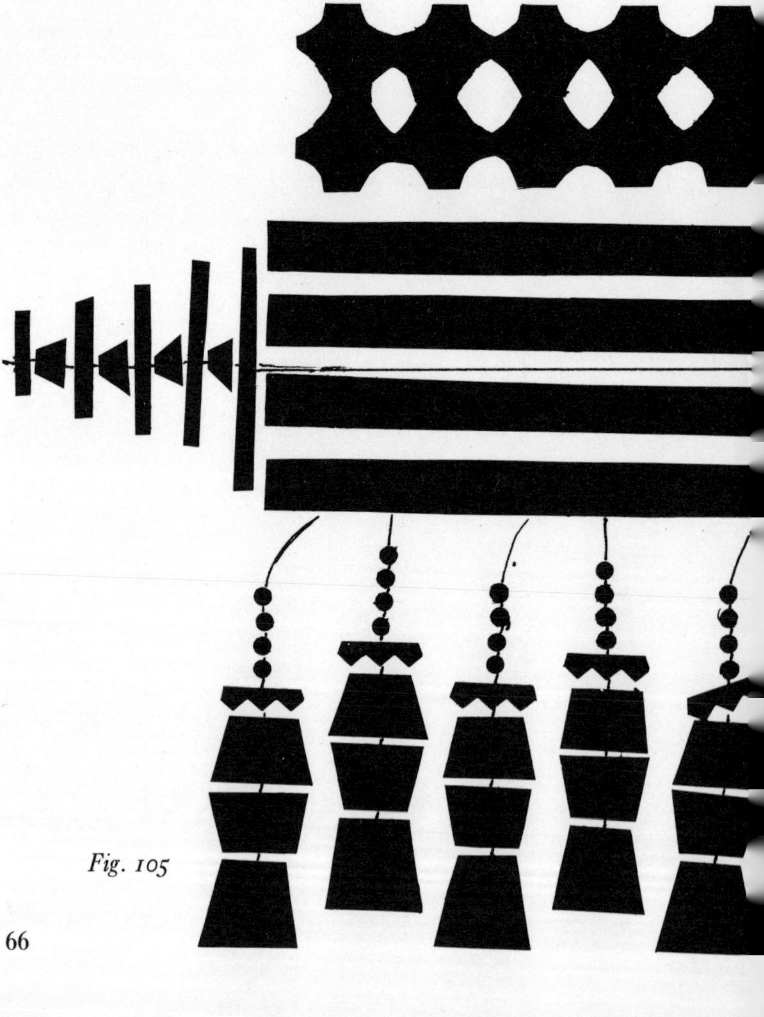

Fig. 105

2. Pass the thread through the body and through a plastic lid. Stick this lid to the body. Also stick the last lid of the tail section to the body.

3. Follow the threading chart, Fig. 105, ending with the plastic lid of the container. Make a large knot and secure to inside of the lid with adhesive. Put lid on the container (head). Add any further details such as bottle tops and pipe cleaners, and frayed thread for beard.

To perform Suspend head and body separately.

Klik-a-Lek

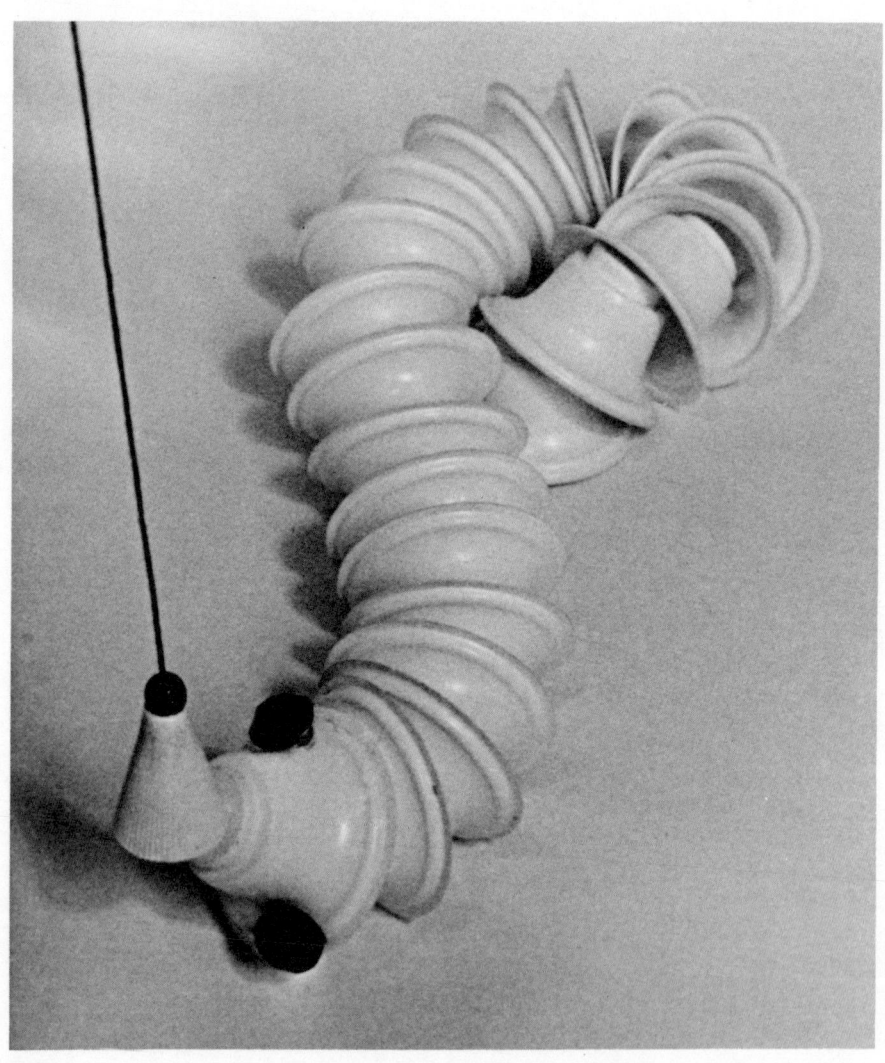

Materials required See Fig. 106. One piece of strong thread 36 in. (90 cm.) long.

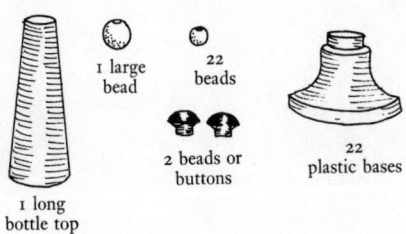

1 long
bottle top

Fig. 106

To make Tie a large bead on to end of thread and thread on the plastic bases alternately with a bead, ending with a plastic base, Fig. 107. Make a knot after threading on each plastic base. Thread on a bottle top and a bead for nose. Stick on the beads or buttons for eyes.

To perform This creature can make a variety of strange sounds according to the speed with which it is moved. Or it can be made to catch its own nose.

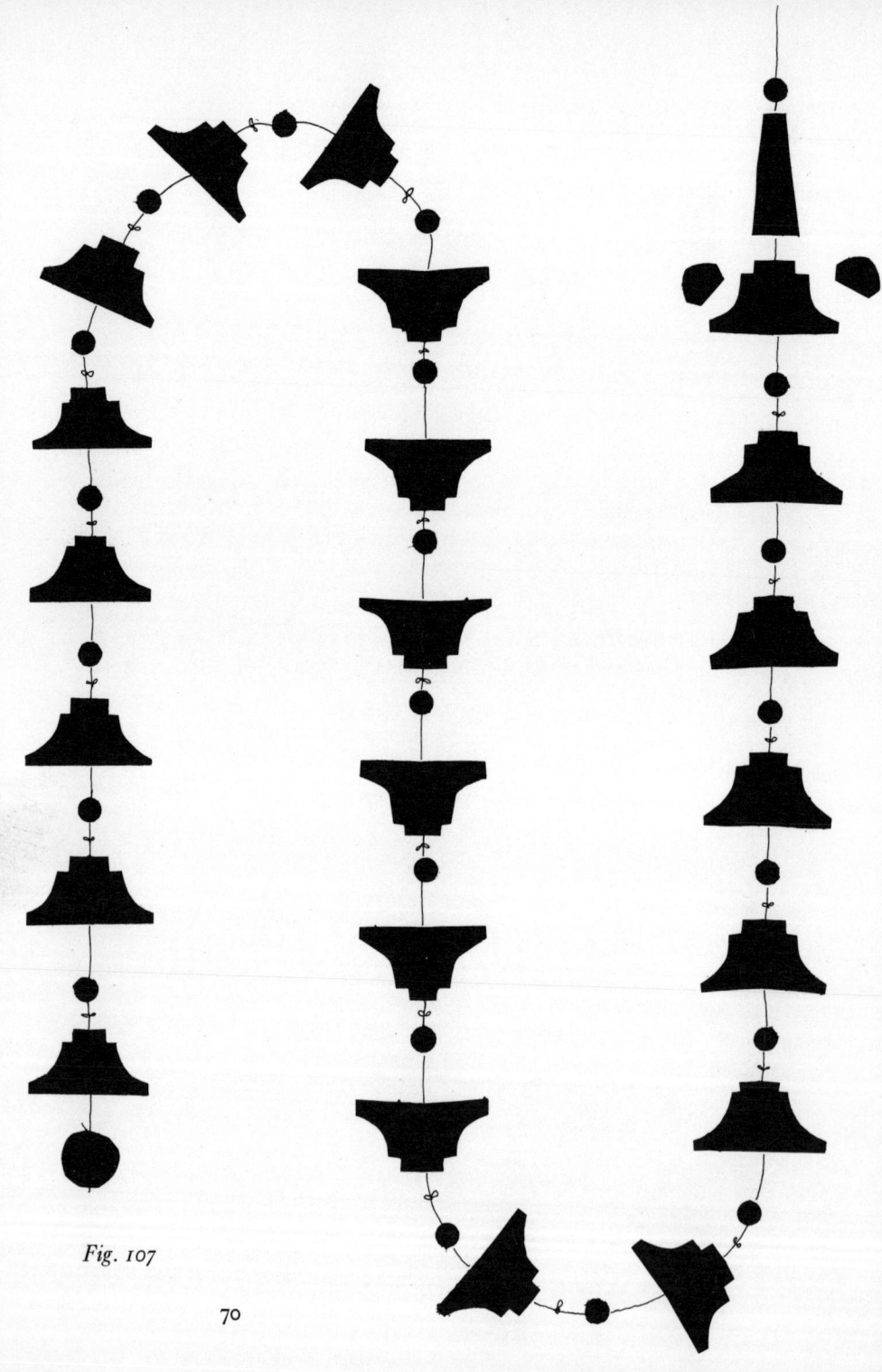

Fig. 107

Snake

A long, creeping creature, which can be raised up from the ground and which provides sounds, can be fun to make.

A long length of thin string or thick thread can be used for threading on an interesting collection of beads, bottle tops, egg-cartoon sections, etc., as in Fig. 108.

Knots are used to keep the pairs of bottle tops apart.

The head should be weighted by placing bottle tops inside the egg-carton sections before joining together.

Colour may be added by using nylon net (fruit containers from the stores) to cover the egg-carton sections, or paint may be used. Pipe cleaners can be used on the head, and a length of black thread should be attached to the point of the head for performance.

Many variations can be developed on this theme. The head and neck from Verti-Brek could be used for part of a snake-like creature.

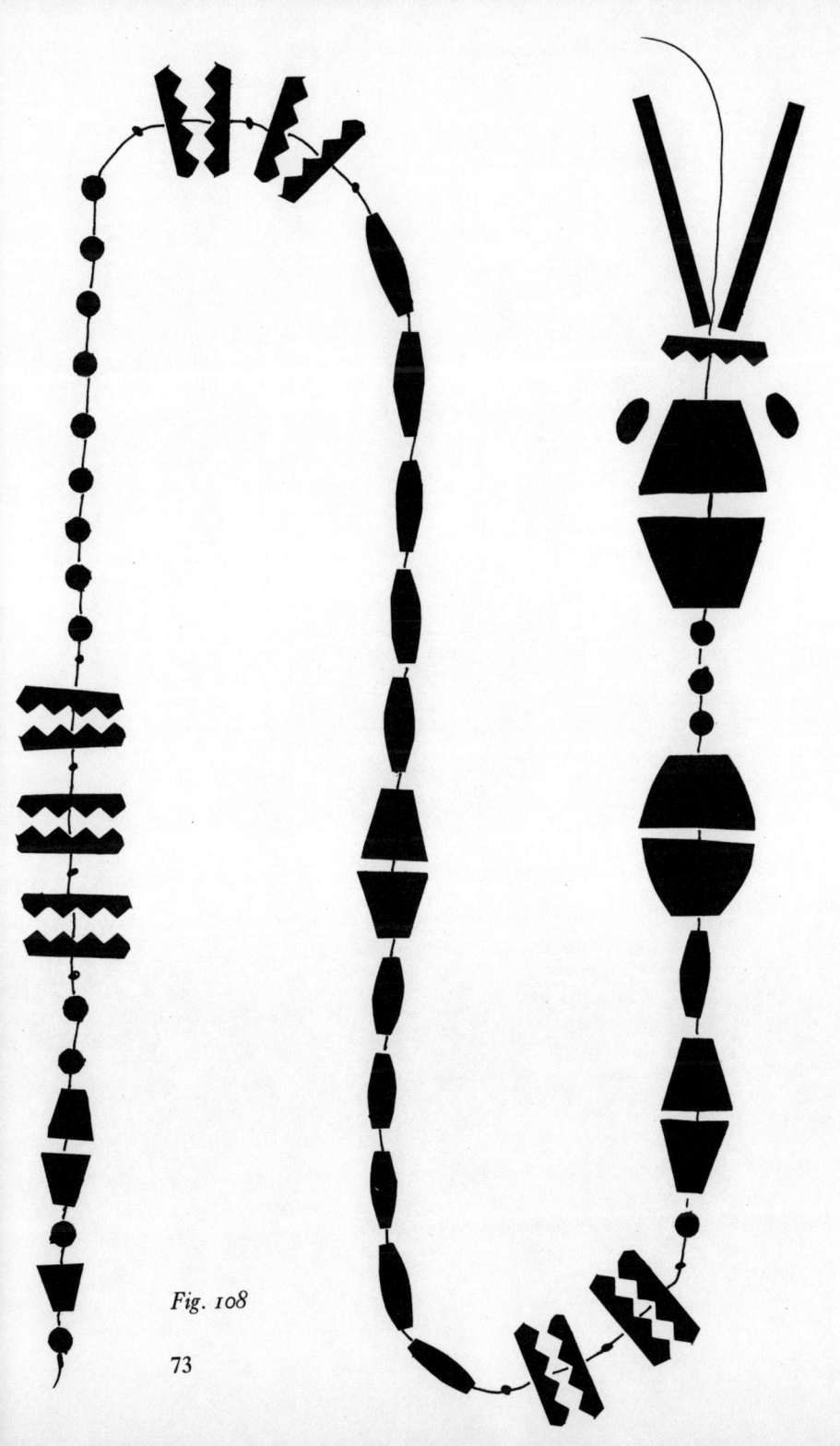

Fig. 108

73

Red-Lek

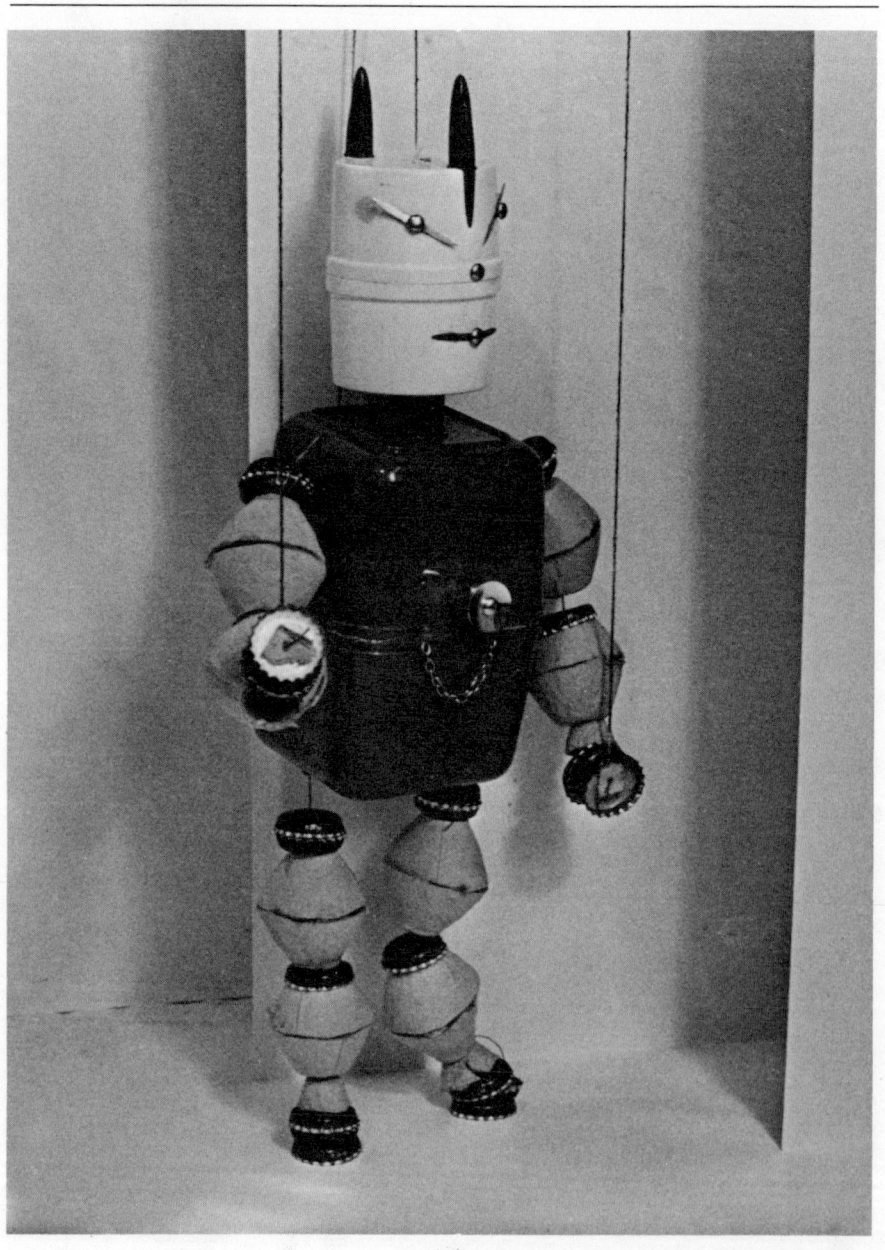

Red-Lek is a rather heavy-looking form of Spaceman and he could be used as a space guard in a play. His features give the appearance of a very severe type of person.

Materials required

See Fig. 109. Five lengths of thread each 18 in. (45 cm.) long.

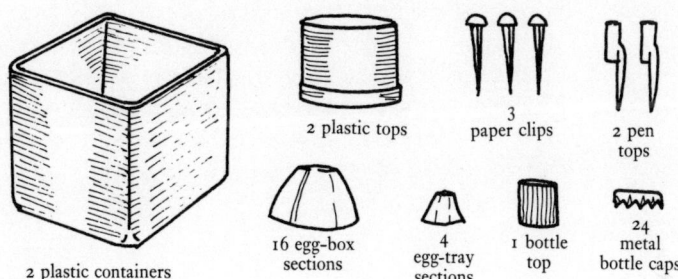

2 plastic tops   3 paper clips   2 pen tops

16 egg-box sections   4 egg-tray sections   1 bottle top   24 metal bottle caps

2 plastic containers

Fig. 109

To make
Arms and Legs

1. Put large knot on end of thread and thread on three bottle caps, Fig. 110a.
2. Thread on small egg-tray section, Fig. 110b.
3. Thread on two egg-box sections and stick together, Fig. 110c.
4. Thread on a bottle cap, and then a pair of egg-box sections which should be stuck together. Fig. 110d.
5. Thread on two bottle caps. Fig. 110e.

This completes one leg or arm. Make four alike.

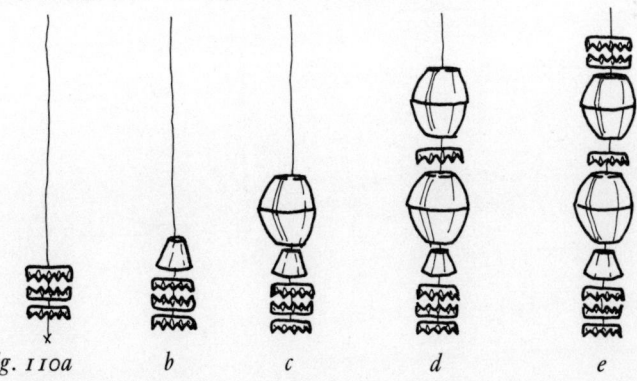

Fig. 110a   b   c   d   e

Body and Head

1. Make two holes, one in each side of container, for legs, Fig. 111a.
2. Make a hole in top and one on each side in the other container, Fig. 111b.

75

3. Thread the leg thread through the container and tie the other leg on to this thread, Fig. 111c.

4. Thread arm thread through the other container and secure the second arm to this thread, as for the legs.

5. Put knot on the other length of thread and bring up through the top of the container. Stick the two body sections together.

6. Thread on a bottle top for neck, and secure with adhesive. Add the two plastic tops to make a head, Fig. 111d.

7. Open out the paper clips for eyes and mouth and stick into position, Fig. 111e. Use just the knob of the paper clip for the nose. Stick on the two pen tops, one at the front of the head and the other at the back.

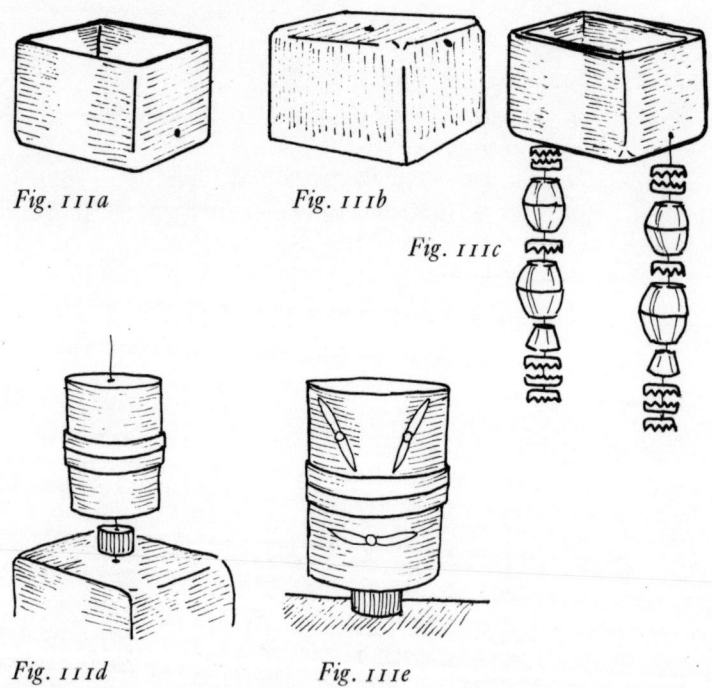

Fig. 111a   Fig. 111b

Fig. 111c

Fig. 111d   Fig. 111e

Note   The front of the body may be decorated with a bottle top. This puppet was called Red-Lek because the body was made from a red container and red bottle tops. Other colours could just as well be used. To perform, see pages 131–140.

76

Fig. 112

Mini-Aut

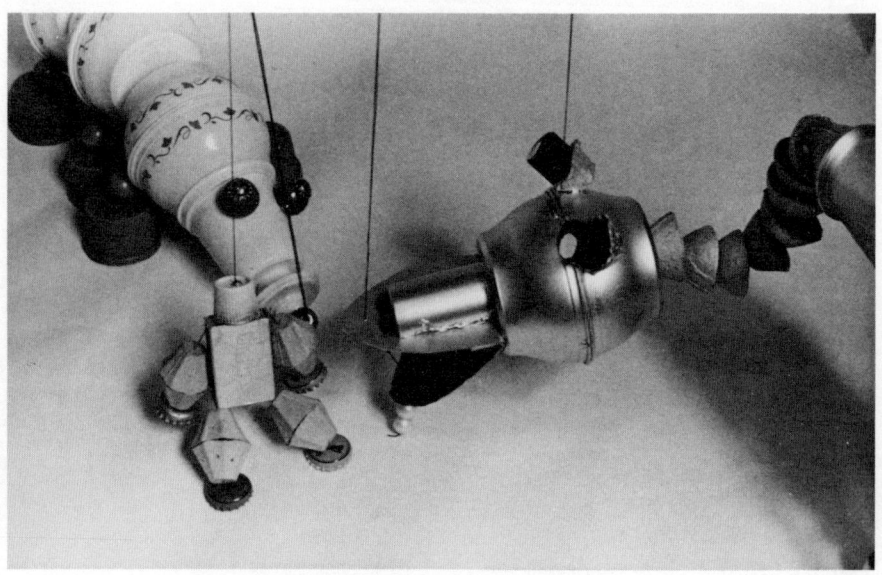

Clockwise: Mini-Aut, Kwok and Aero-Lek

Materials required   See Fig. 113. Four lengths of thread each 12 in. (30 cm.) long.

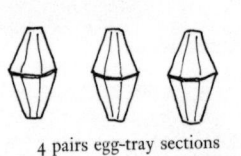

1 match box

4 pairs egg-tray sections

1 bottle top

4 bottle caps

Fig. 113

To make
Limbs

1. Put a knot on the end of thread and thread on a bottle cap, Fig. 114a.
2. Thread on an egg-tray section, Fig. 114b.
3. Thread on an egg-tray section and paste to previous one, Fig. 114c.

This completes one limb. Make four limbs.

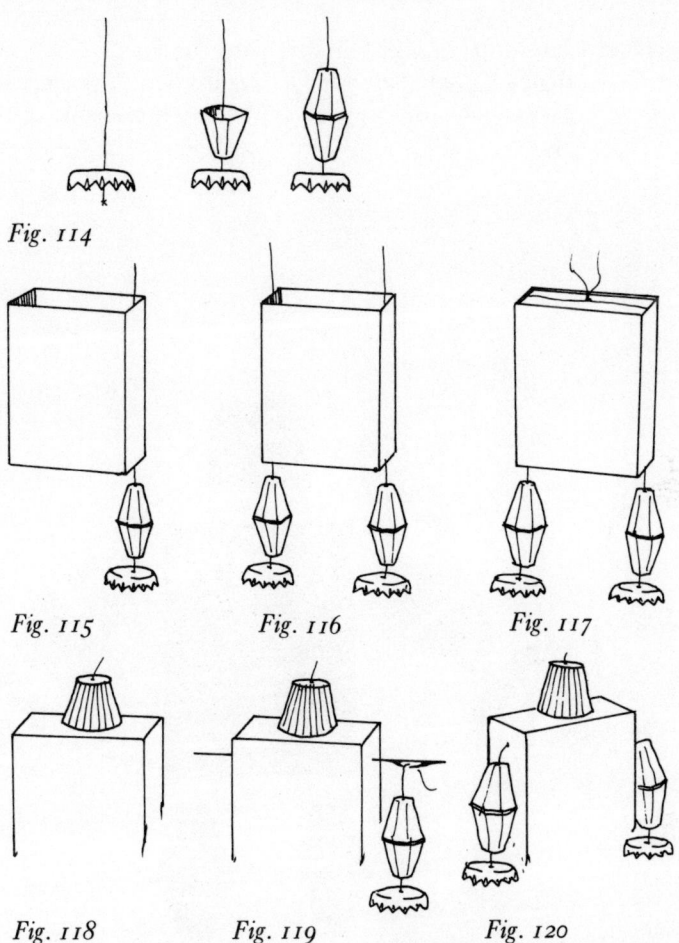

Fig. 114

Fig. 115   Fig. 116   Fig. 117

Fig. 118   Fig. 119   Fig. 120

To assemble

1. Remove inside of matchbox, Fig. 115.
2. Pass the thread of one limb through the box and stick at top and bottom, Fig. 115.
3. Attach a second limb, Fig. 116.
4. Push matchbox together and tie threads together, Fig. 117.
5. Pass threads up through a bottle top and stick top securely to top of matchbox, Fig. 118.
6. Pass a limb thread through the eye of a needle.
7. Push needle through side of the matchbox, Fig. 119.
8. Tie the two arm-limb threads together, Fig. 120, and put a spot of adhesive on the knot to prevent it coming apart.

79

To perform Use only a single thread from the head. The movements will depend upon the speed of raising and lowering. This creature gives a splendid impression of weightlessness, or the antics of a clown.

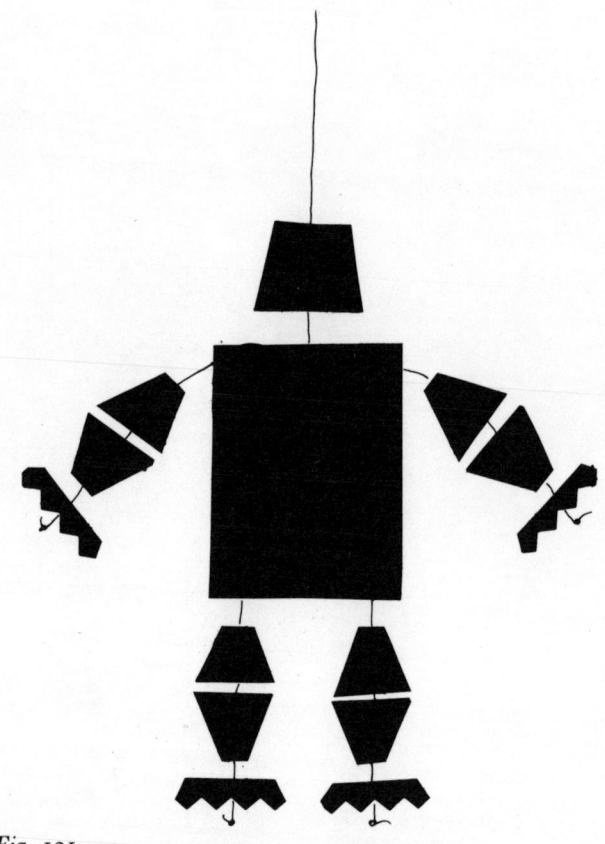

Fig. 121

Midi-Aut

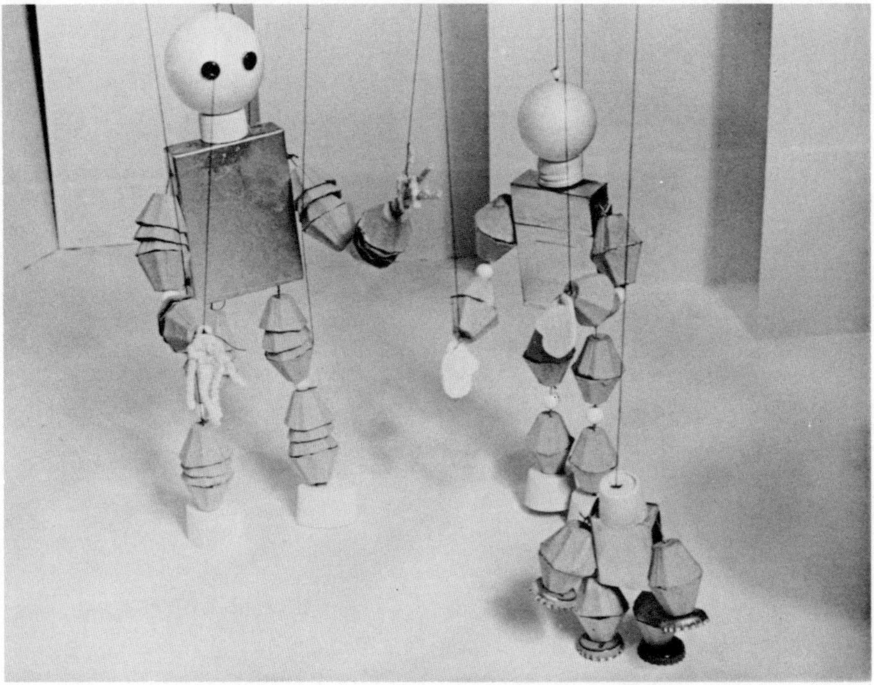

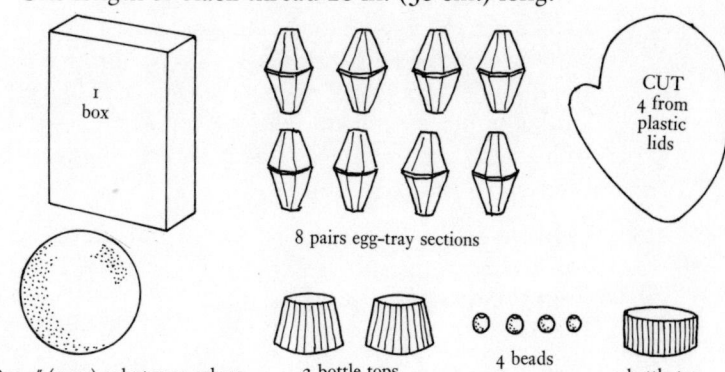

Clockwise: Maxi-Aut, Midi-Aut and Mini-Aut

Materials required

See Fig. 122. Four lengths of thread each 16 in. (40 cm.) long. One length of black thread 20 in. (50 cm.) long.

Fig. 122

1 box

8 pairs egg-tray sections

CUT 4 from plastic lids

One 2″ (5 cm) polystyrene sphere

2 bottle tops

4 beads

1 bottle top

To make

Legs 1. Put a knot on end of thread and thread on a bottle top, Fig. 123a.
2. Thread on an egg-tray section, Fig. 123b.
3. Thread on another egg-tray section, Fig. 123c, sticking this to the previous one.
4. Put a knot on the thread and thread on a bead, Fig. 123d.
5. Make another knot and thread on an egg-tray section, Fig. 123e.
6. Thread on another egg-tray section, sticking it to the previous one, Fig. 123f.

Make a second leg the same way.

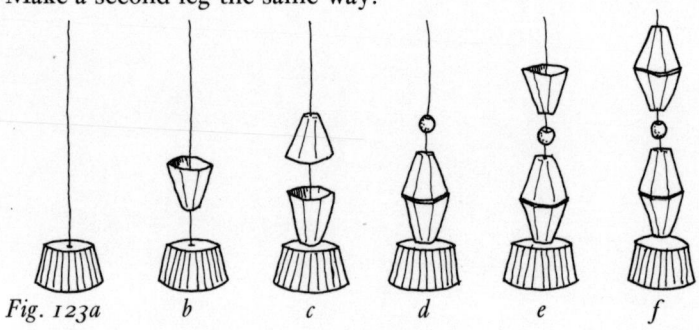

Fig. 123a b c d e f

Hands These are made from white plastic lids. If there is a lot of printing on the lids, stick two lids together to hide it.
1. Thread a plastic hand on to the thread, and tie into position.
2. Make a knot and make the arms the same as for the legs (Fig. 123b–f), following instructions 2 to 6.

Body Make two holes in base of box for legs, and one in top for neck. Make two more holes in the side for arms. Thread the leg strings up through the hole in the base and up through the neck. Put a knot in the string near to the box, Fig. 124. Thread arms strings through the box and knot the string near the base, then tie on the other arm to this thread. Cover knot with adhesive and cut off ends of thread, Fig. 125.

Neck and head Thread on a bottle top for neck, Fig. 126, and then a polystyrene sphere. Stick the sphere to bottle top, Fig. 127. (It may be necessary to cut away a little of the sphere to make a flat base for attaching the neck.)

Attach arms and head to control (see page 127).

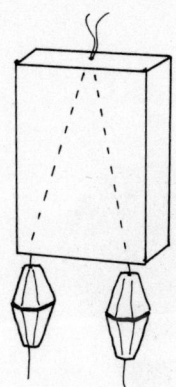

Fig. 124

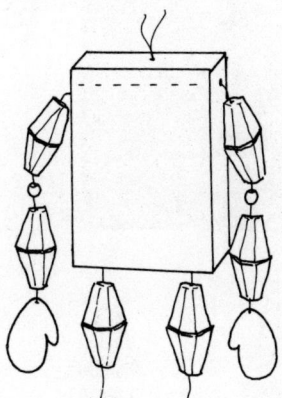

Fig. 125

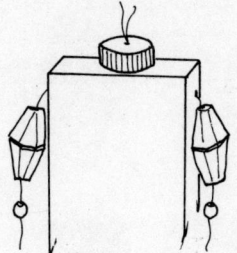

Fig. 126

83

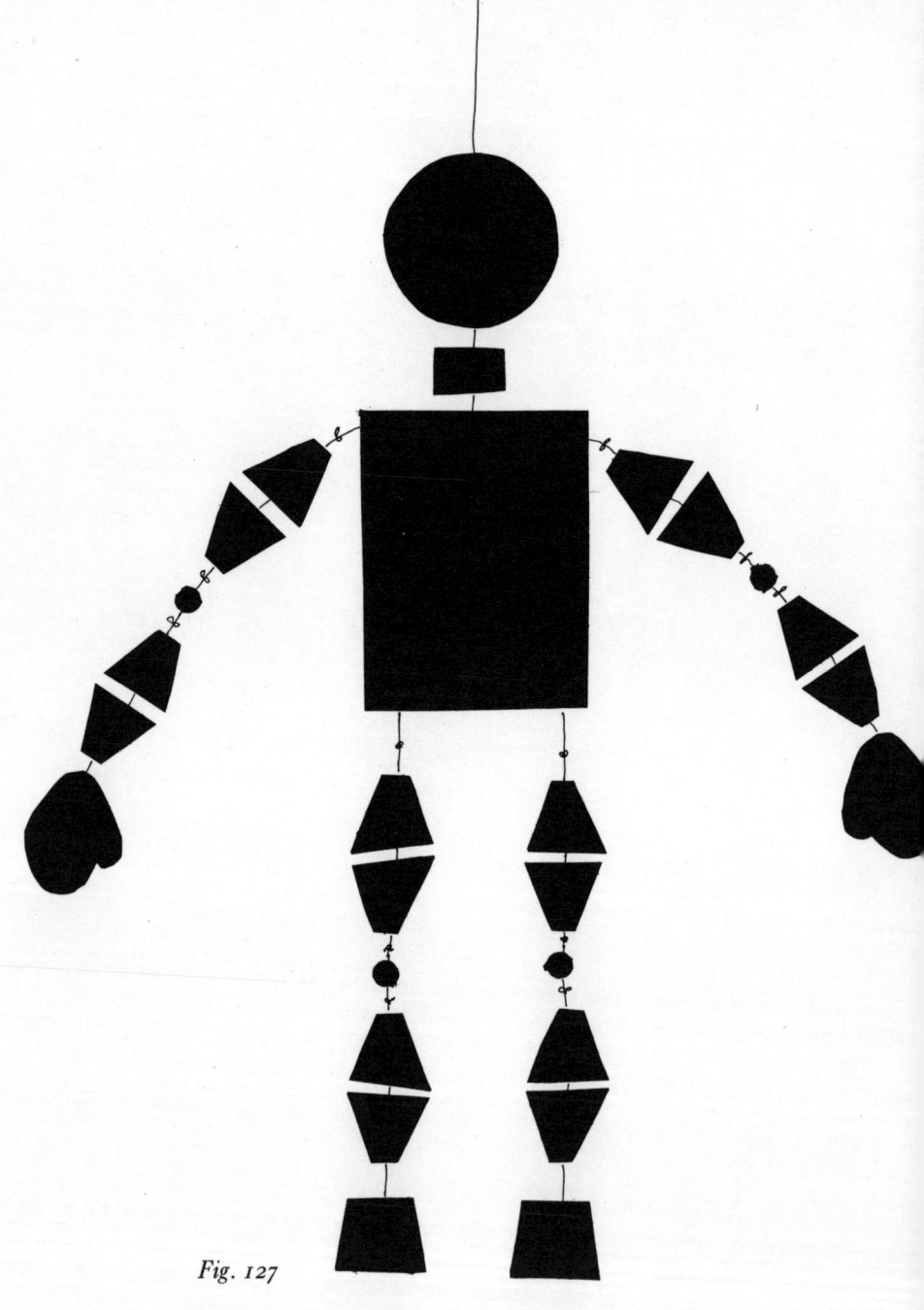

Fig. 127

84

Maxi-Aut

Materials required   See Fig. 128. Four lengths of thread each 18 in. (45 cm.) long. One length of thread 30 in. (76 cm.) long.

A 3″ (7·5 cm) polystyrene sphere

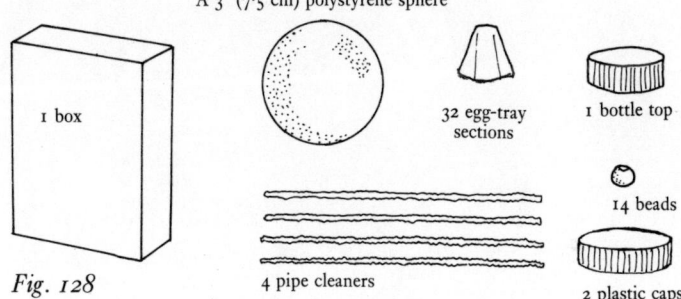

1 box

32 egg-tray sections

1 bottle top

14 beads

Fig. 128   4 pipe cleaners

2 plastic caps

Preparation Spray the box with paint.

To make
Legs

1. Make two holes in the plastic cap, Fig. 129a.
2. Pass the thread down through the egg-tray section (using a needle threaded with thread), Fig. 129b.
3. Pass thread down through the plastic cap, Fig. 129c.
4. Bring the thread back up through the cap and egg-tray section, Fig. 129d.
5. Thread the two ends of thread through a needle, and bring up through egg-tray section, Fig. 129e. Then stick the two sections together.
6. Thread on a bead and another egg-tray section, Fig. 130a.
7. Thread on another egg-tray section, Fig. 130b. This may be stuck to the previous one.
8. Thread on a bead and two egg-tray sections, Fig. 130c.
9. Thread on a bead and two egg-tray sections as before, Fig. 130d.

This completes one leg. Make a second leg.

Fig. 129a   b   c   d   e

85

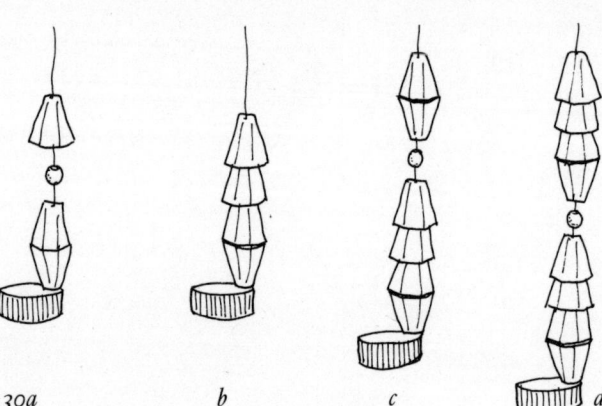

Fig. 130a   b   c   d

Arms

1. Thread on a bead and tie at end of thread.
2. Thread on egg-tray sections as for legs, Figs. 129b to 130d.

Make a second arm.

Hands

Cut off a third of the length of the two pipe cleaners, Fig. 131a. Bend the two larger pieces in half, Fig. 131b. Using one of the smaller pieces, intertwine the two halves together to form four fingers and join on the remaining small piece for a thumb, Fig. 131c, d and e. Attach to arm string.

Make a second hand, and attach in the same way.

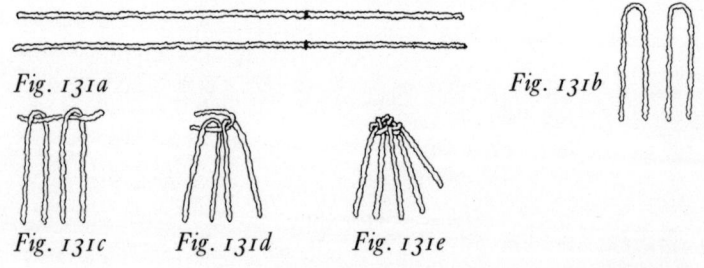

Fig. 131a   Fig. 131b

Fig. 131c   Fig. 131d   Fig. 131e

Body

For the body and making up, follow instructions for the Midi–Aut on page 82.

To perform The fingers may be bent round a small piece of cane to represent a recorder or other wind instrument. This puppet may also wear a cloak and be made to play the piano.

There is great scope for the development of this puppet and the various types of action.

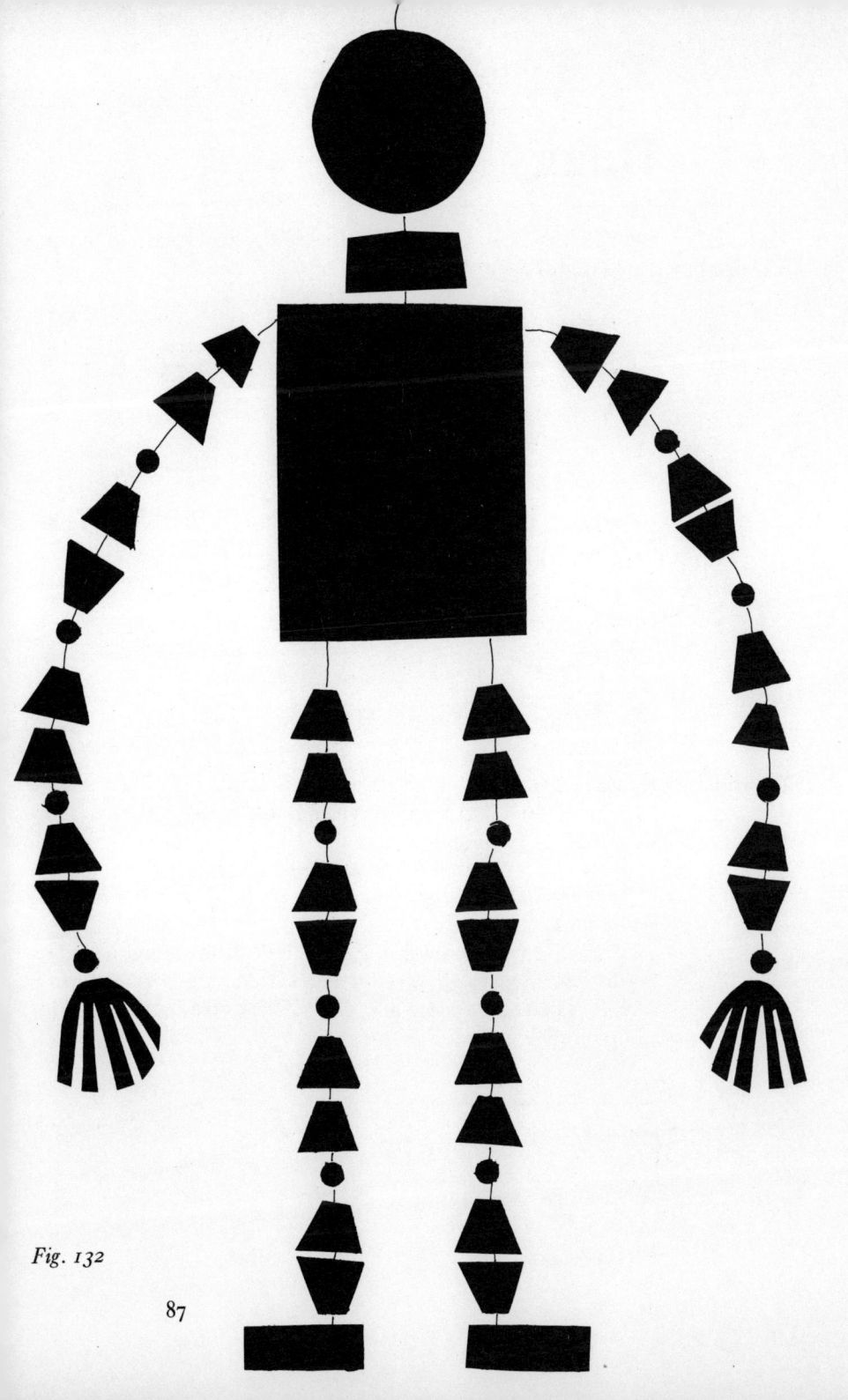

Fig. 132

Buggy

Materials required   See Fig. 133. Two pieces of cardboard to equal length of box and $\frac{1}{2}$ in. (1 cm.) deeper than side of box.

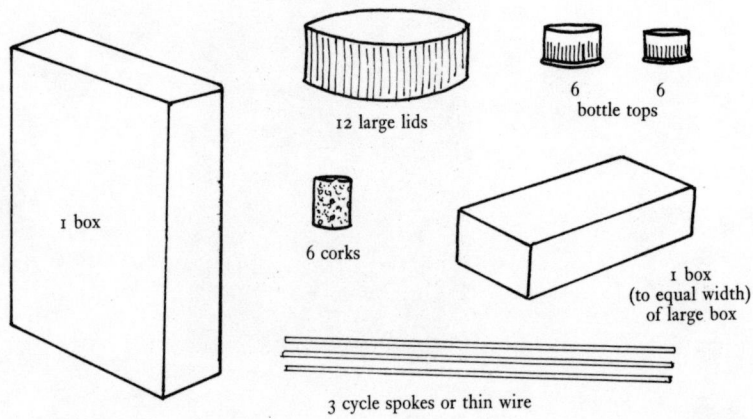

12 large lids

6   6
bottle tops

6 corks

1 box

1 box
(to equal width)
of large box

3 cycle spokes or thin wire

Fig. 133

To make   1. Make three holes in the two pieces of cardboard. These should be $\frac{1}{4}$ in. (5 mm.) up from lower edge and spaced evenly. They should be large enough to take the wire, Fig. 134.
2. Stick the cardboard to the sides of box, Fig. 135.
3. Make holes in the centre of the twelve lids and in the six small bottle tops.
4. Thread a wire through the front holes and thread on first a bottle top, then two large lids (stick these together to form a wheel). Then add a piece of cork and stick on a bottle top. This completes one wheel, Fig. 136.

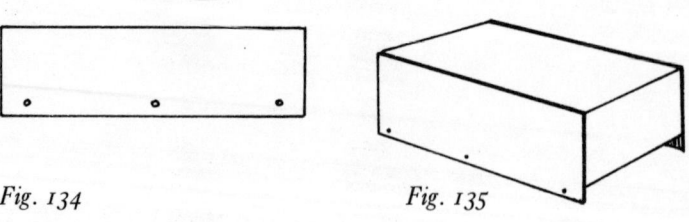

Fig. 134   *Fig. 135*

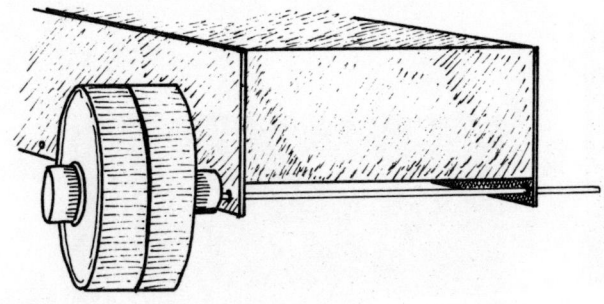

Fig. 136

5. Make a second wheel in the same way, but cut the wire if it is too long.

6. Attach all wheels.

7. Stick on a box to form a seat and add any controls, according to the use of the buggy.

To perform Suspend all four corners of the box to a control, Fig. 137.

The buggy should move along easily and in a performance one of the monsters could easily give it a push.

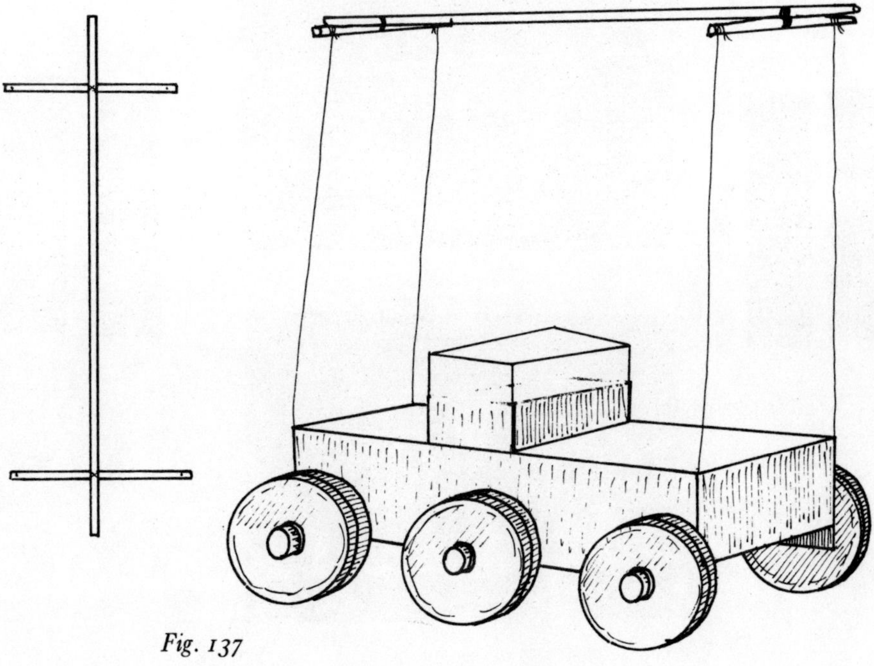

Fig. 137

Fig. 138

Conductor

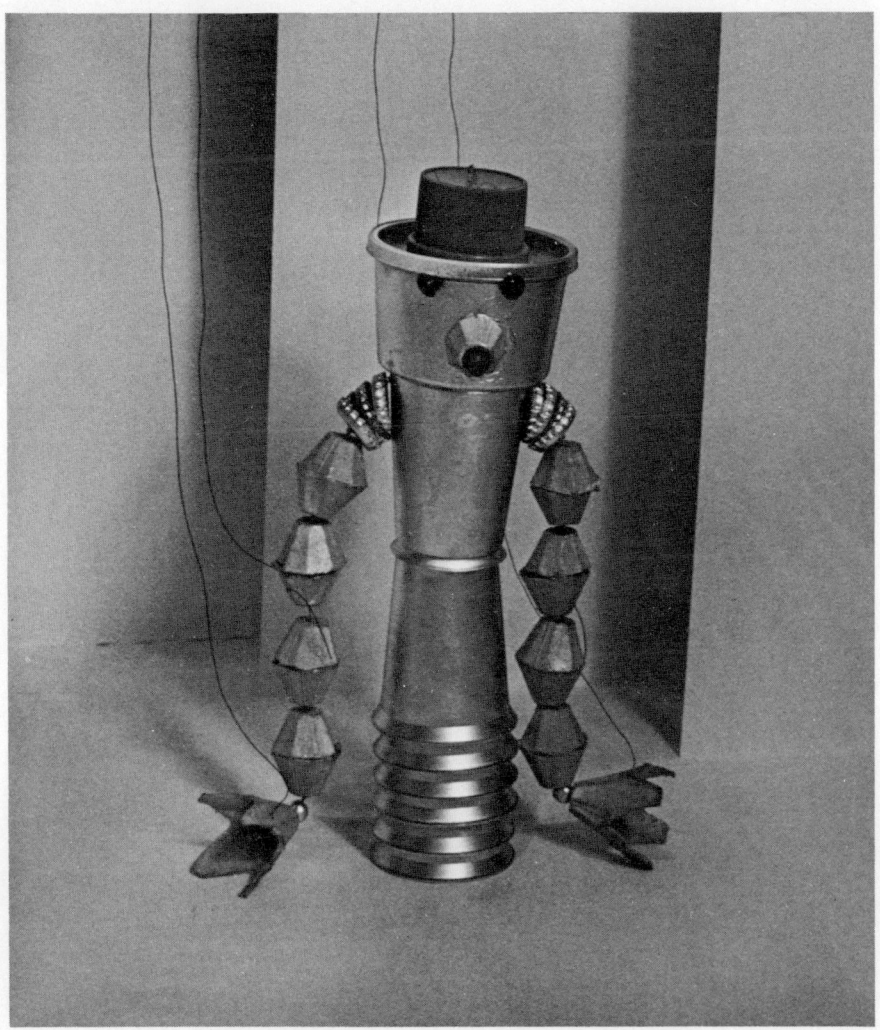

This figure has a great number of interesting arm movements which are fascinating to watch. The body can contract and gradually expand during the course of the performance.

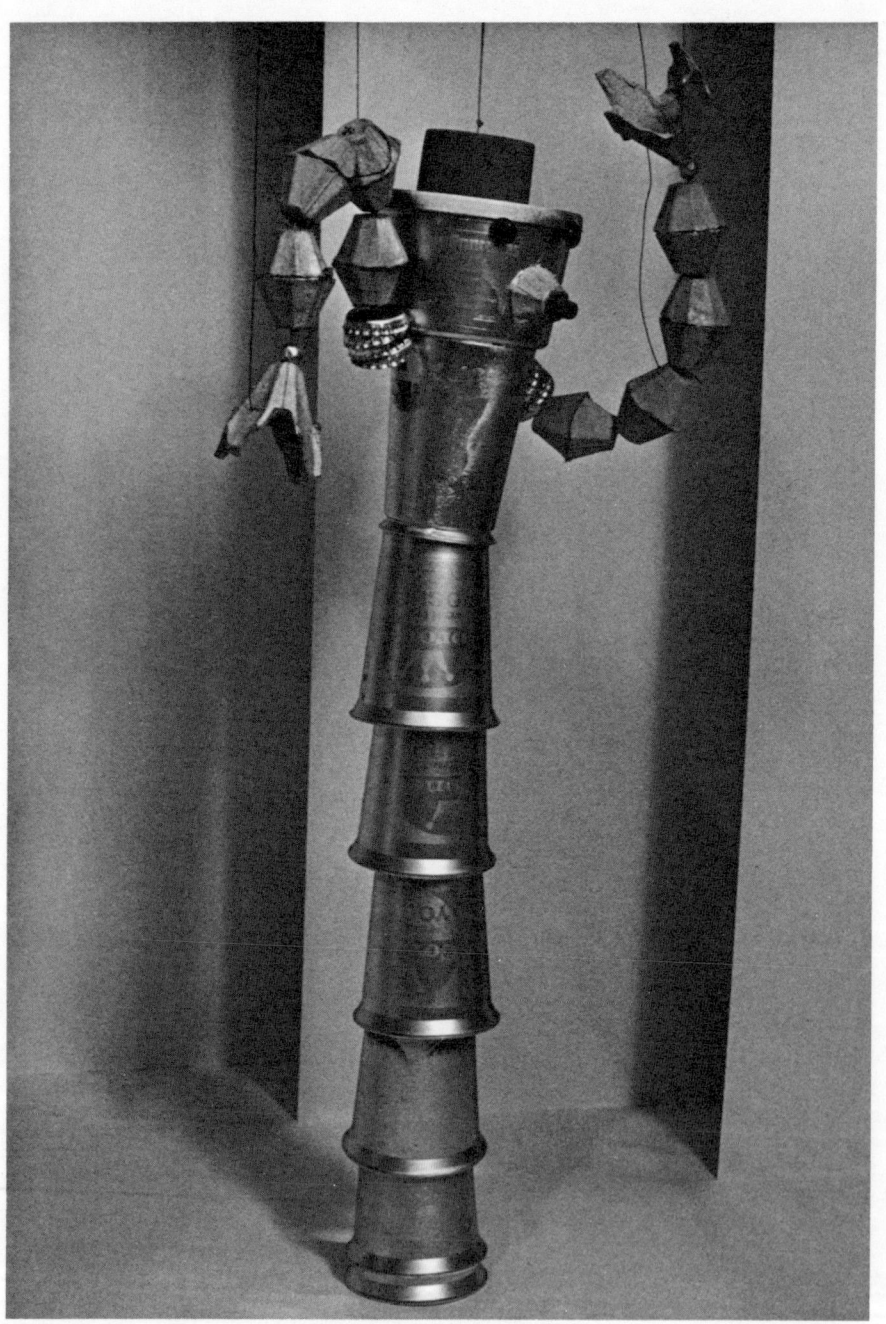

| **Materials required** | See Fig. 139. Two lengths of thread each 18 in. (45 cm.) long. One length of thread 36 in. (90 cm.) long. |

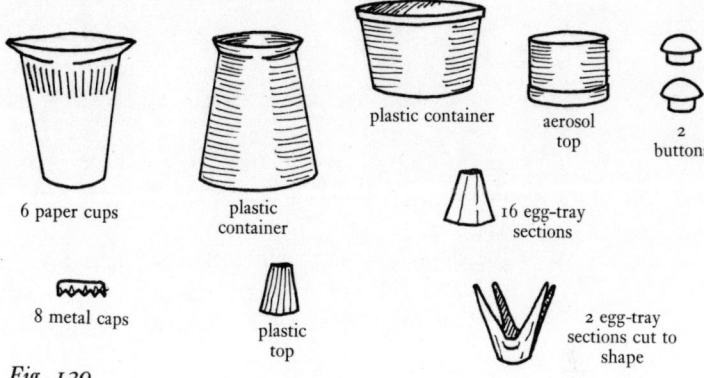

Fig. 139

To make

Arms

1. Make a knot in the end of thread and thread on an egg-tray section cut to shape (this is the hand) Fig. 140a.
2. Make a knot, then thread on a pair of egg-tray sections, Fig. 140b. Stick the two sections together. Repeat this stage until there is a total of four pairs of egg-tray sections, then thread on four bottle tops.
3. Make another arm in the same way.
4. Make two holes, one on each side of the plastic container, Fig. 141a, and thread through one of the arm threads. Join the second arm to this thread, Fig. 141b.

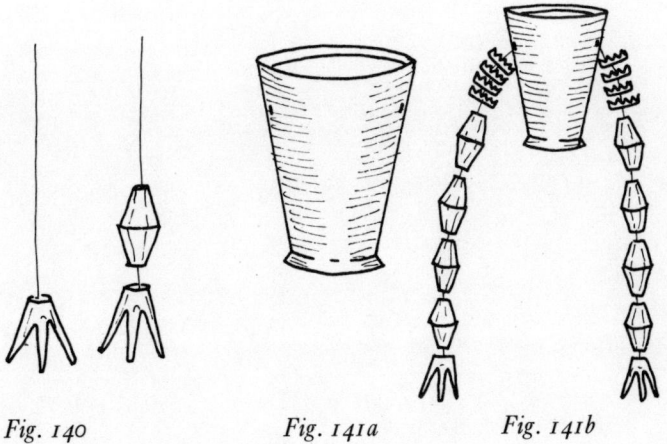

Fig. 140   *Fig. 141a*   *Fig. 141b*

93

Body

1. Put knot on to the end of thread, and thread on a paper cup, Fig. 142a.
2. Make a very large knot about 2 in. (5 cm.) away from the base of cup, Fig. 142b.
3. Thread on another cup, Fig. 142c.

Continue making knots and threading on cups until all the cups are on.

4. Pass the thread up through the plastic container, with arms already on. Join the last cup and this container together with adhesive.
5. Thread on a plastic container for face and stick to body. Thread on an aerosol lid and stick in position. Stick on buttons for eyes and a top for nose, Fig. 143.

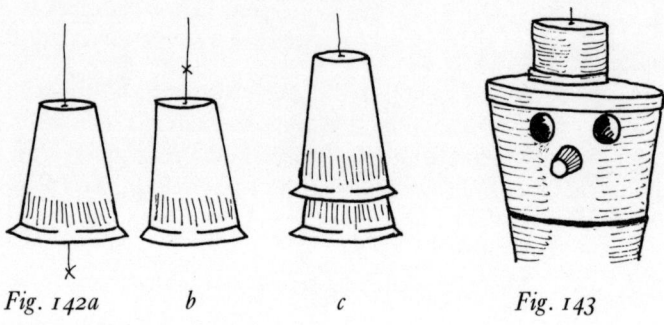

Fig. 142a   b   c   Fig. 143

To perform Suspend from top of head. The arms can be on a separate control.

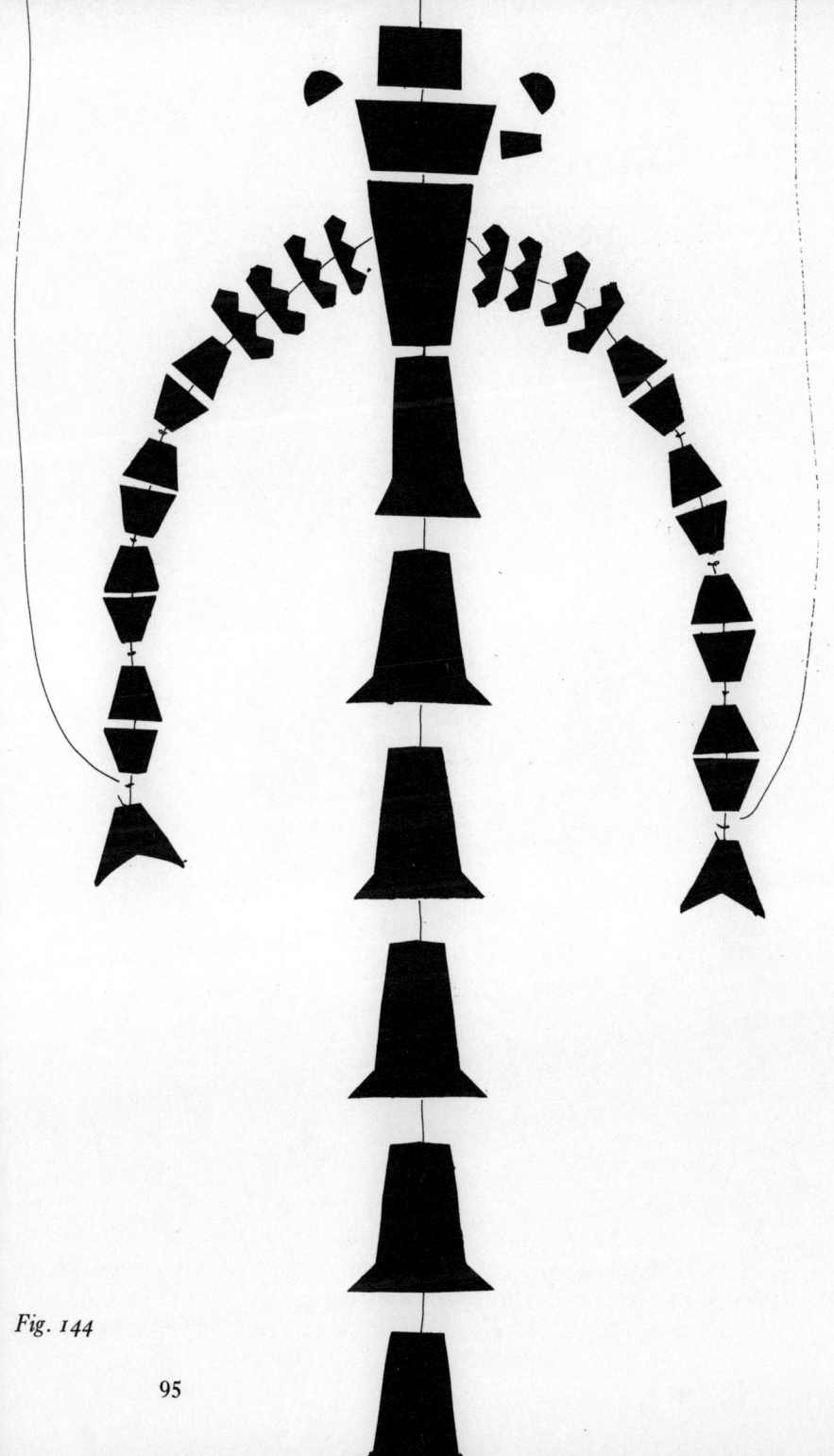

Fig. 144

95

Dancer

This figure is very flexible and a great variety of interesting movements can be obtained by moving the arms or legs. A circle of transparent fabric can be draped around the lower part of the

figure, and then most of the movement can be made with the arms.

The figure is silent, so that the flexibility of the movement is more important.

Materials required   See Fig. 145. Four lengths of thread each 15 in. (38 cm.) long. One length of thread 24 in. (60 cm.).

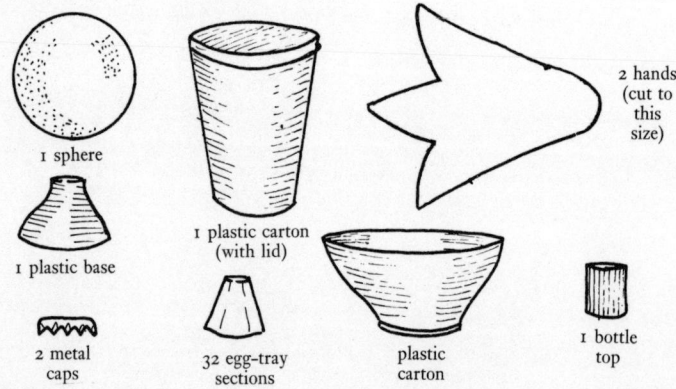

1 sphere

1 plastic base

1 plastic carton (with lid)

2 hands (cut to this size)

plastic carton

1 bottle top

2 metal caps

32 egg-tray sections

Fig. 145

To make

Arms

1. Secure a hand to end of thread, Fig. 146a.
2. Thread on a pair of egg-tray sections, Fig. 146b.
3. Stick the sections together and make a knot in the thread, Fig. 146c.

Thread on three more pairs of egg-tray sections, making a knot between each pair.

This completes one arm. Make a second arm.

4. Make a hole in each side of the plastic container, Fig. 147. Thread through one arm thread and tie the other arm thread to it, Fig. 148.

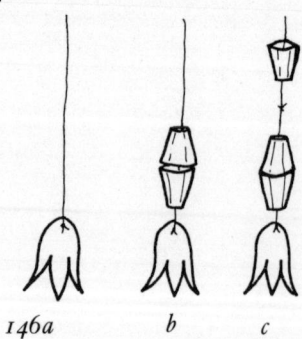

Fig. 146a   *b*   *c*

98

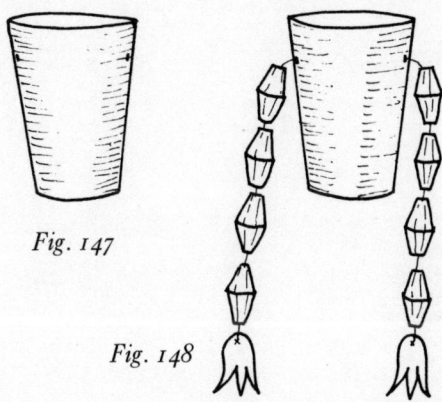

Fig. 147

Fig. 148

Legs

1. Make a knot in end of thread and thread on bottle cap, Fig. 149a.
2. Cut two pointed foot shapes from the plastic lid, Fig. 149b, and thread one of these on to the thread, Fig. 149c.
3. Make up as for arms.
4. Make two holes in base of plastic container, Fig. 150. Thread the leg threads through and tie securely, Fig. 151. Note: egg-tray sections should show below container.

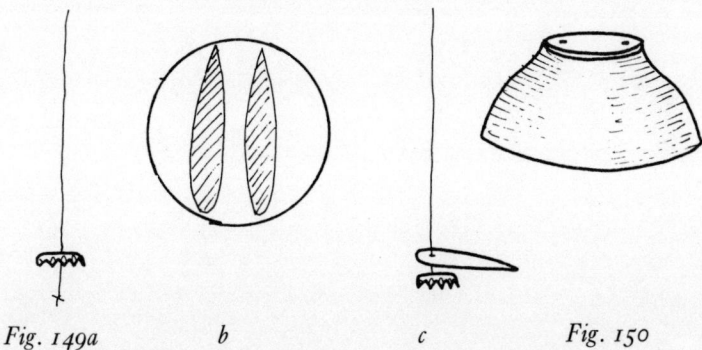

Fig. 149a   b   c   Fig. 150

Body and head

1. Put a knot on to the end of thread and thread through the various containers as in Figs. 152 and 153. Stick together.
2. Use the bottle top for the neck and a polystyrene sphere for the head. Features can be added, using beads, sequins or even small buttons.

99

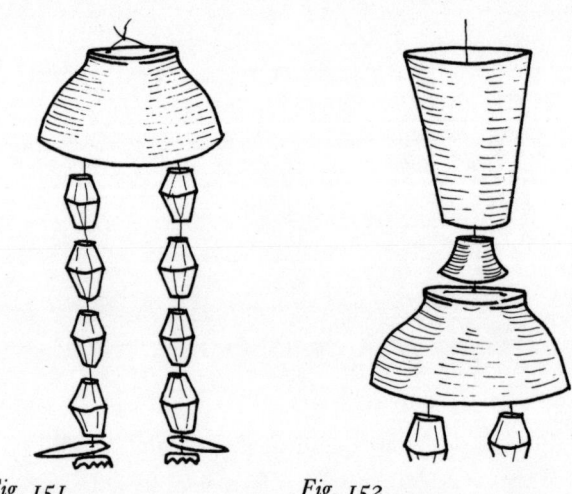

Fig. 151   *Fig. 152*

To perform This puppet should be strung on a cross bar with a bowing string.
Legs may not be suspended but left loose, but if the legs are
required for movement, then a separate control may be made.

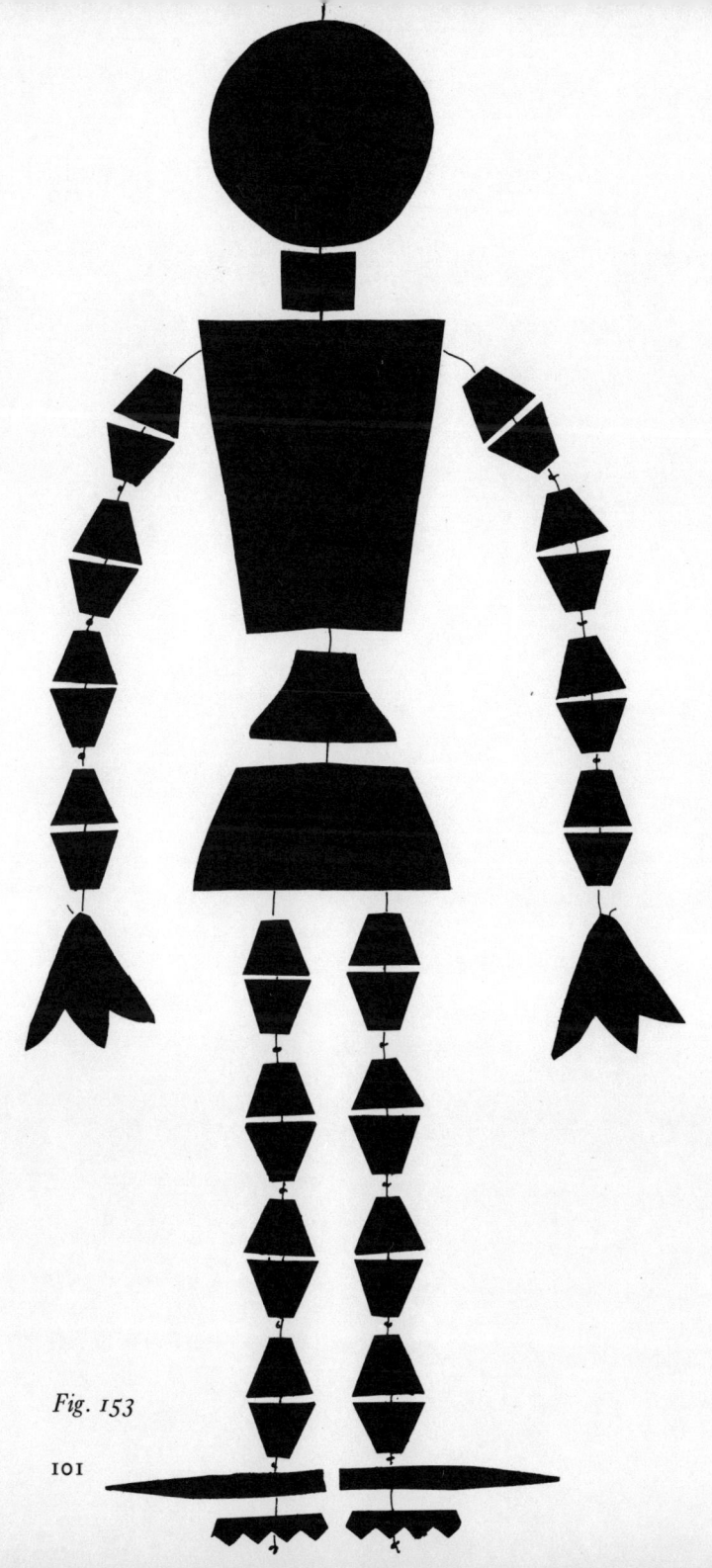

Fig. 153

101

Three Little Dancers

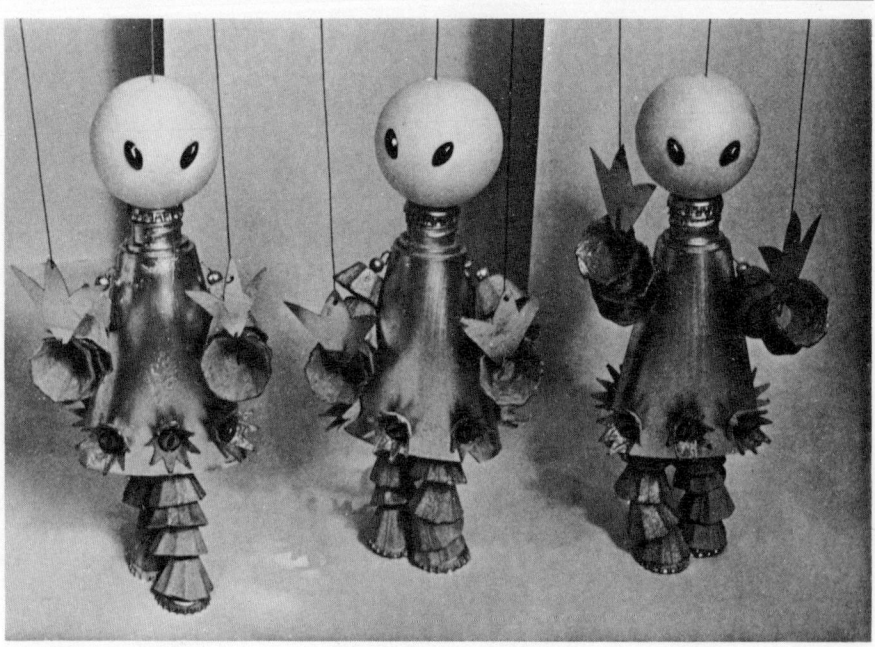

Materials required

For each puppet:
See Fig. 154. Four lengths of string 12 in. (30 cm.) long. One length of string 24 in. (60 cm.) long.

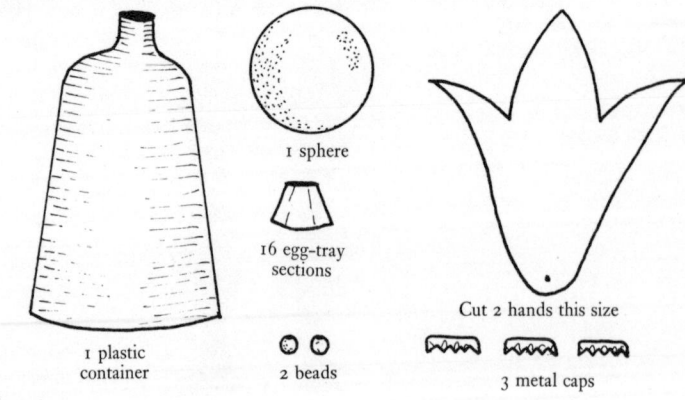

1 sphere

16 egg-tray sections

Cut 2 hands this size

1 plastic container

2 beads

3 metal caps

Fig. 154

Preparation Using a bradawl, make holes in the ends of egg-tray sections and in the metal caps. Cut along the lower edge of the plastic container so that it is hollow.

To make

Legs   1. Knot one end of string, then thread through a bottle cap, Fig. 155a. Thread on an egg-tray section, Fig. 155b, and glue to bottle cap. Put knot in thread about $\frac{1}{4}$ in. (5 mm.) away, Fig. 155b.
2. Thread on an egg-tray section and put a knot in thread, Fig. 155c.
3. Thread on another egg-tray section and put a knot in thread, Fig. 155d.
4. Thread on another egg-tray section and put a knot in thread, Fig. 155e.

This completes one leg.

Make a second leg.

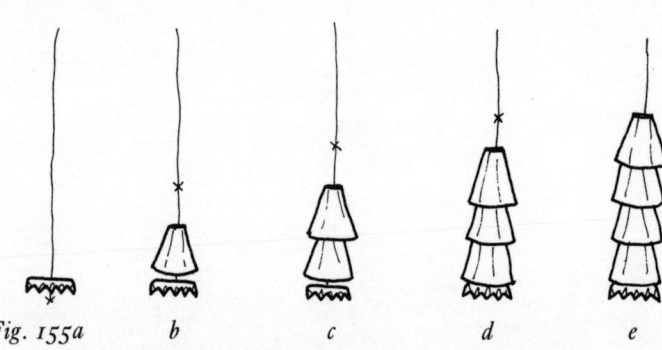

Fig. 155a   *b*   *c*   *d*   *e*

Arms

1. Tie string onto hand and put a knot about $\frac{3}{4}$ in. (2 cm.) away from hand, Fig. 156a.
2. Thread on an egg-tray section and put a knot in thread as before, Fig. 156b.
3. Thread on an egg-tray section and put a knot in thread as before, Fig. 156c.
4. Thread on an egg-tray section and repeat as before, Fig. 156d.
5. Cut the next egg-tray section to make it smaller, then thread onto thread, Fig. 156e.
6. Put a knot in the thread and attach a bead, making a knot to secure, Fig. 156f.

This completes one arm. Make a second arm.

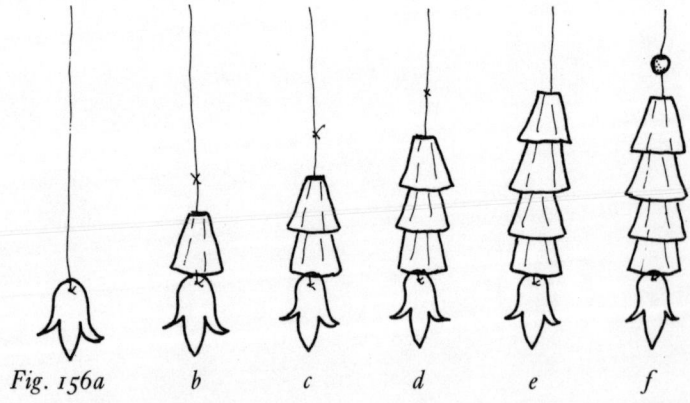

Fig. 156a   *b*   *c*   *d*   *e*   *f*

Attaching arms and legs

1. Make two holes near to the top of the plastic container. Thread through one arm (using a needle), Fig. 157.
2. Tie the second arm to the first one, Fig. 158. Put a little adhesive on the knot to make it secure.

3. Cut a small oval-shaped piece of cardboard, Fig. 159.
4. Thread the leg threads through the cardboard, and tie together, Fig. 160.
5. Secure a length of thread to the centre of the oval card and pass the thread up through the body, Fig. 161. Pass up through a metal bottle cap, Fig. 161.
6. Pull up the thread so that the legs show as in Fig. 162. Secure the top thread with a knot and some adhesive.
7. Make a hole through the polystyrene sphere and thread on to the body thread, Fig. 162. Secure the head with adhesive. Eyes may be added by using beads or sequins.

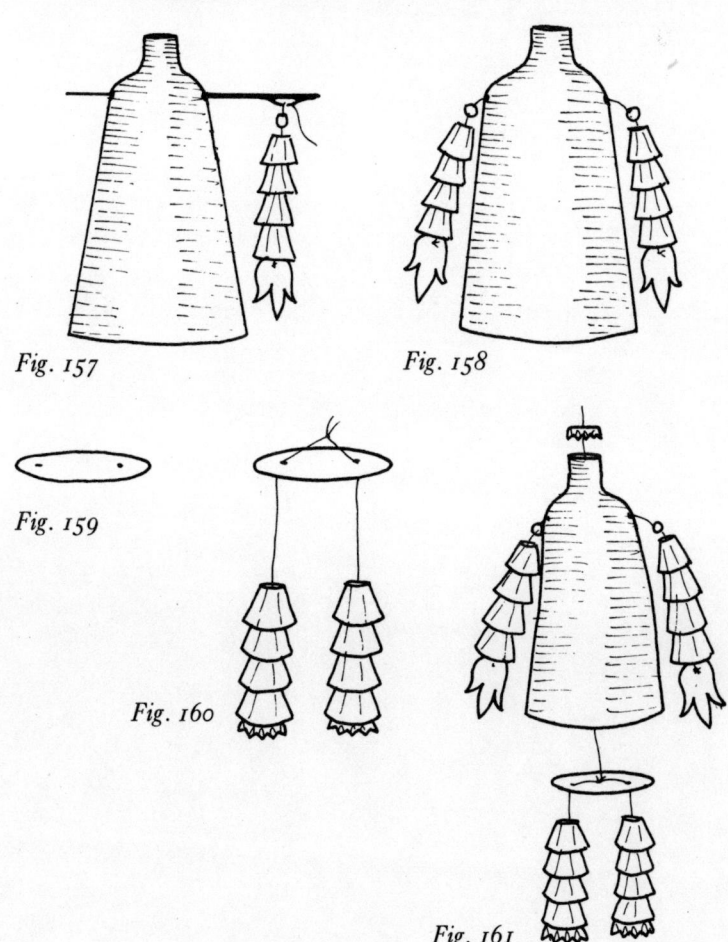

Fig. 157

Fig. 158

Fig. 159

Fig. 160

Fig. 161

Fig. 162

Dress   The dress may be decorated with egg-carton sections cut to
obtain a serrated edge and a button stuck into the flat portion,
Fig. 164 (see also photograph on page 102).

The flying type of dancer has a circle of transparent fabric
attached to the figure. The diameter of the circle should equal
the width of puppet, with arms outstretched. The circle is cut
down towards the centre and opened out so that the centre of
the circle is attached to the neck and the tips of the circles to the
hands, Fig. 163.

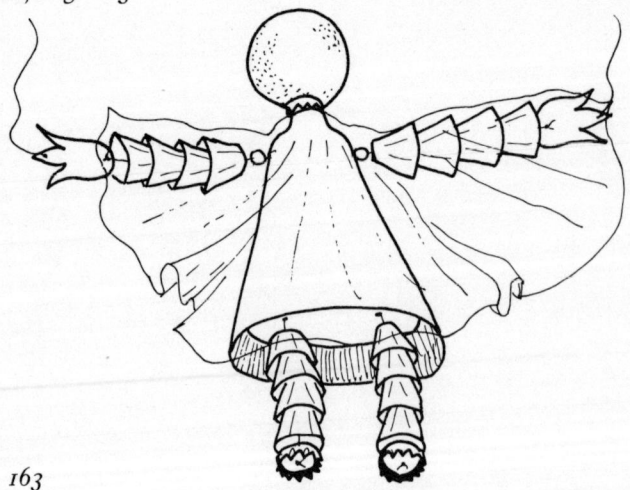

Fig. 163

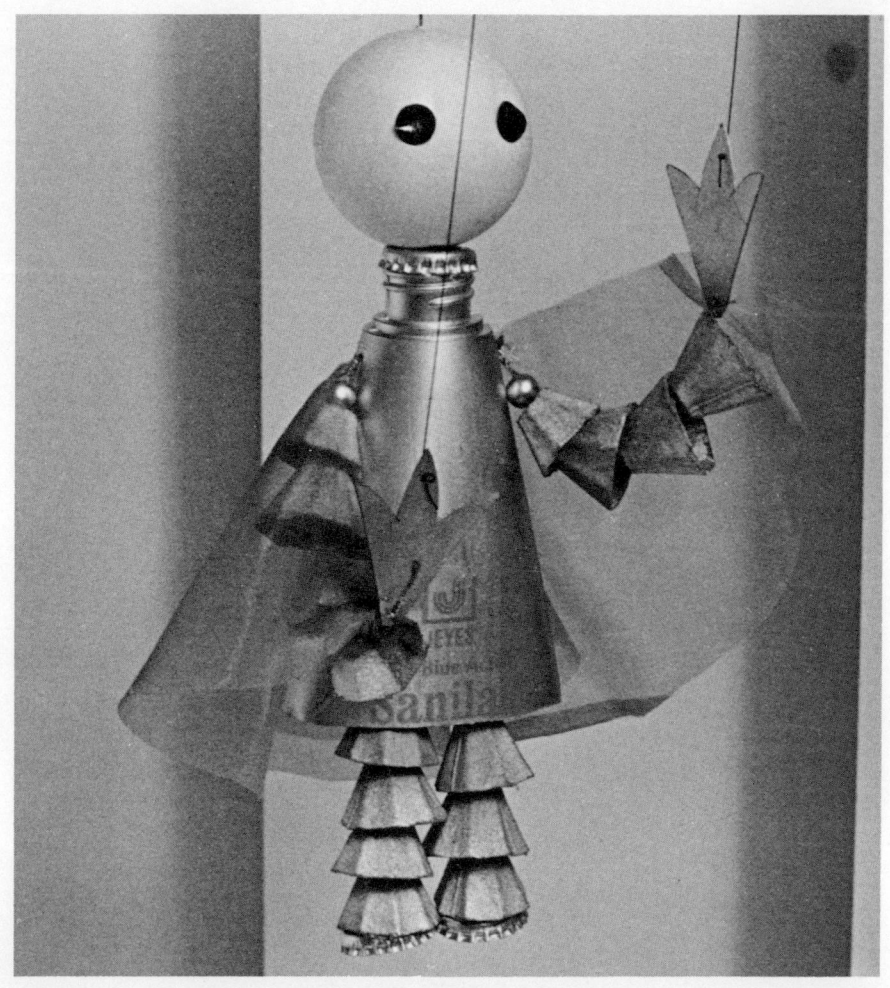

Note　　　For three dancers, make three separate figures and attach to two
separate rods, i.e. all the heads to one rod and all the hands to
the other.

To perform See pages 131–140.

Fig. 164

Earth People

Sue and Jim belong to the planet Earth and these puppets can be dressed in fabrics. The styles of dress can be anything which you may wish to create.

SUE

Materials required

One piece of foam sheeting $4\frac{1}{2}$ by $7\frac{1}{2}$ in. (12 by 19 cm.) for body. Four pieces foam sheeting $2\frac{3}{4}$ by $\frac{1}{2}$ in. (7 by 1·5 cm.) for legs. One piece foam sheeting $2\frac{1}{2}$ by $\frac{1}{2}$ in. (7 by 1·5 cm.) for neck. Two pieces non-fray fabric each 6 by $1\frac{1}{2}$ in. (15 by 4 cm.) for legs. One piece thin fabric 5 by 5 in. (13 by 4 cm.). Two pieces string each 10 in. (26 cm.) for arms. Two plastic bottle tops about $1\frac{1}{4}$ in. (3 cm.) in diameter, for feet. One piece non-fray fabric 7 by 2 in. (18 by 5 cm.) for hands. One 3 in. (7·5 cm.) polystyrene sphere. Two pearl beads.

To dress

Two pieces of fabric each 8 by 12 in. (20 by 30 cm.)—non-fray is best. Weights are required in hands and feet—flattened lead shot or heavy washers.

To make

Legs

1. Take a length of non-fray fabric, fold in two, and oversew the end, Fig. 165a.
2. Place a piece of foam sheeting inside and oversew edges together, Fig. 165b.
3. Run-stitch across to make knee joint, Fig. 165c.
4. Place another piece of foam inside and oversew, Fig. 165d.
5. Draw ends together and thread on a pearl bead, and a bottle top, Fig. 166a.
6. Make a hole in centre of lead shot and thread on, also a scrap of fabric, Fig. 166b.
7. Pass the needle and thread back up through the fabric, shot, bottle top and bead, Fig. 166c.
8. Secure thread to leg fabric, Fig. 166d.

Make a second leg in the same way.

If the legs are too light in weight, add Plasticine to the inside of the bottle tops.

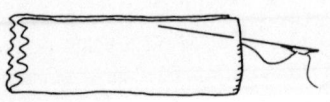

Fig. 165a

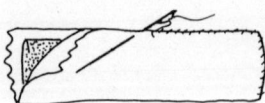

Fig. 165b

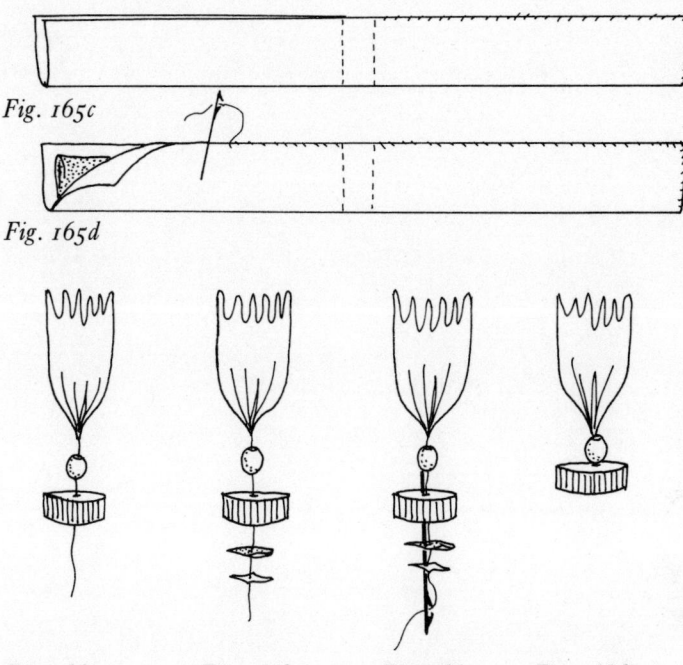

Fig. 165c

Fig. 165d

Fig. 166a   Fig. 166b   Fig. 166c   Fig. 166d

Body

1. Fold body foam in three, Fig. 167a.

2. Cover with thin fabric and oversew (if fabric frays, turn in raw edge). Leave one end open, Fig. 167b.

3. Join partly along the top of body, leaving gap for neck, Fig. 168a. Roll the narrow strip of foam sheeting to form a neck. Wrap a scrap of plain fabric round it, and attach to neck opening of body, Fig. 168b.

4. Secure a long length of thread into the neck, Fig. 168c.

5. Attach the legs to the body, using long stitches, and leave slack. Wrap thread around these stitches to give a little strength, Fig. 169.

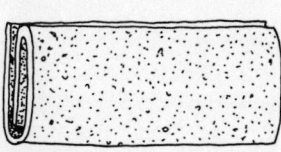

Fig 167a

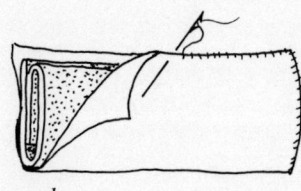

b

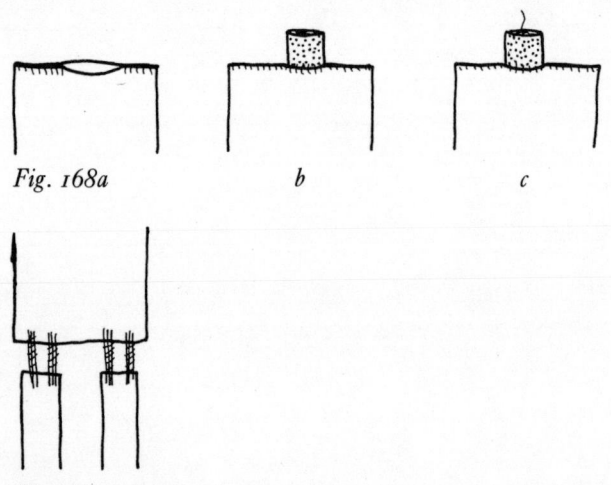

Fig. 168a   b   c

Fig. 169

Head and arms

1. Make a pattern of a hand shape, Fig. 170, about $1\frac{3}{4}$ in. (4·5 cm.) long and $1\frac{1}{2}$ in. (4 cm.) wide.

2. Cut out four hands from the fabric, Fig. 171.

3. Join two hand-pieces together by oversewing, but place a flattened piece of lead shot between the layers, Fig. 172. This gives weight to the hand.

4. Fold one length of string as in Fig. 173 and join together by stitching through the string. Attach a hand to one end of the string, Fig. 174.

5. Attach the arms to the body by stitching the end of the string to the top of the body, Fig. 175.

Head is attached to puppet after it is dressed.

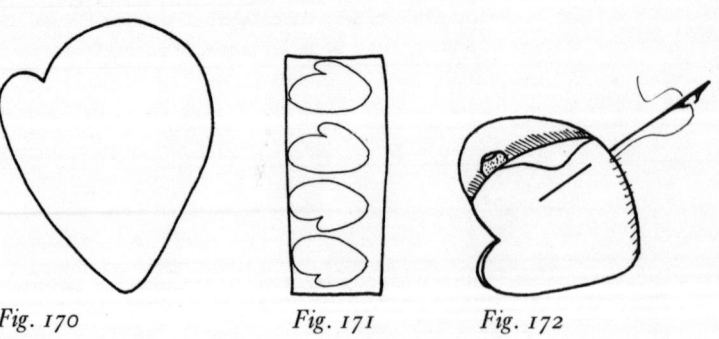

Fig. 170   Fig. 171   Fig. 172

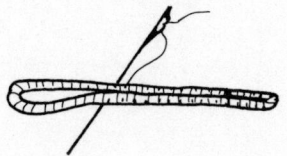

Fig. 173

Fig. 174

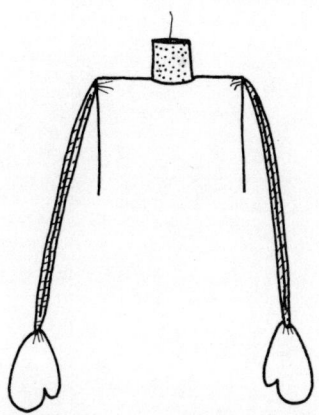

Fig. 175

To dress   1. Make a pattern as shown in Fig. 176. The solid lines are for
the dress worn by Sue.
2. Fold the fabric as in Fig. 177 so that the pattern can be cut out
twice.
3. Place the two right sides of the fabric together and join as in
Fig. 178, leaving a gap for the neck. Turn right side out and put
dress on to puppet.
4. Using a strip of fabric 3 by $1\frac{1}{2}$ in. (8 by 4 cm.), fold as in
Fig. 179a and wrap around puppet neck and stitch into position.
This forms a collar, Fig. 179b.

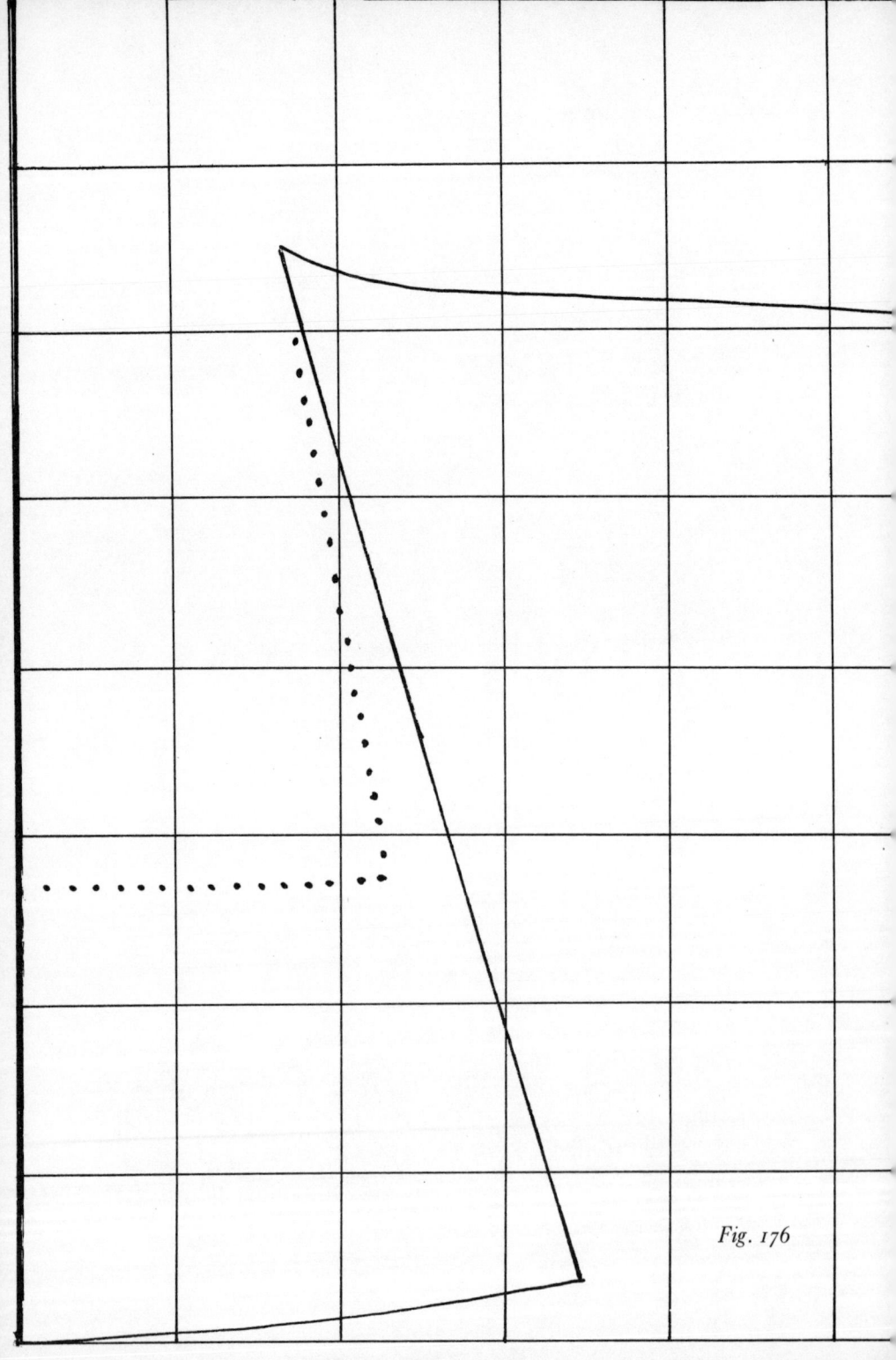

Fig. 176

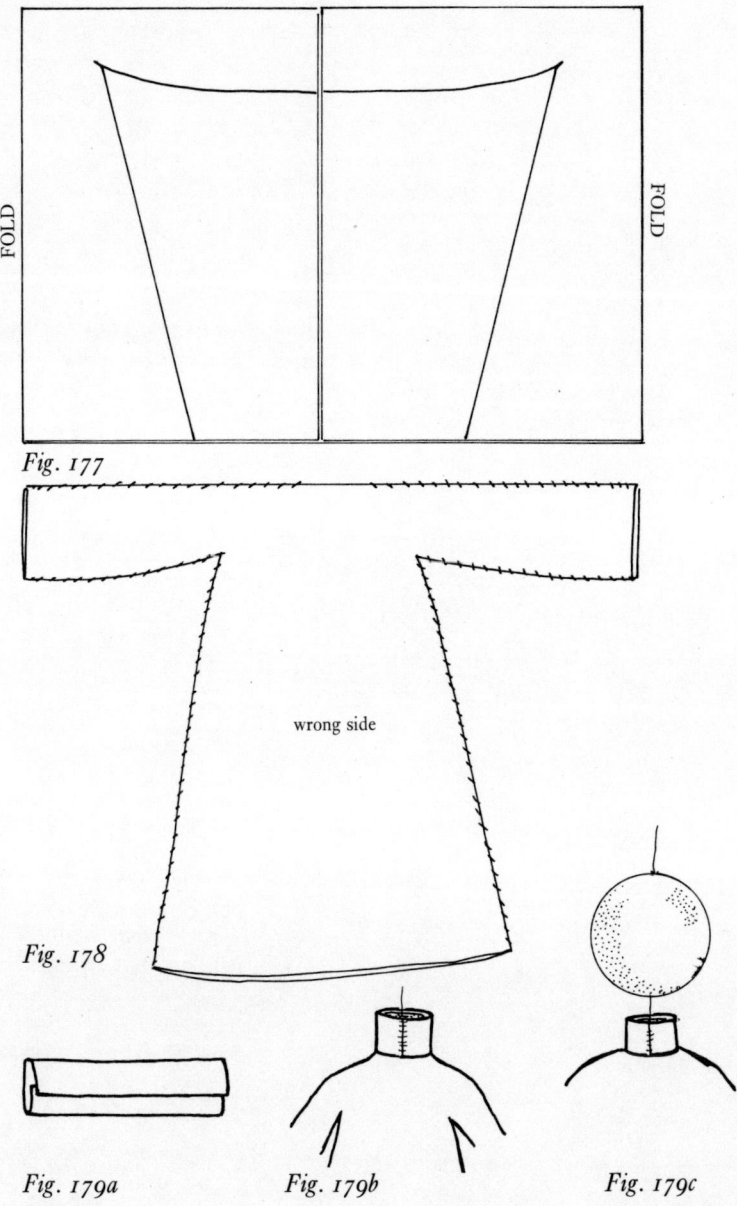

Fig. 177

wrong side

Fig. 178

Fig. 179a　　*Fig. 179b*　　*Fig. 179c*

Head　　Make a hole through the polystyrene sphere and thread on to neck thread, Fig. 179c. Put a spot of adhesive at top of head to make secure.

115

Hair   Hair may be made from a variety of materials. Here are a few ideas:

1. Unravel some loosely woven tweed, but leave in two or three threads to form a parting, Fig. 180a and b. This could form a long, flowing hairstyle, Fig. 181.

2. Wind thick wool or raffia on to a card (this must be equal to length of hair), stitch along the top edge and cut along the lower edge.

This forms a wig, Fig. 182a and b.

3. A piece of non-fray fabric or leather can be cut as in Fig. 183a and b. Place on to the puppet, and trim according to taste. This was used for Jim's hair, Fig. 183c.

Features may be added by using small buttons or beads for eyes.

To perform See pages 131–140.

Fig. 180a   Fig. 180b

Fig. 181   Fig. 182a   Fig. 182b

Fig. 183a   Fig. 183b   Fig. 183c

JIM

Materials required

One piece foam sheeting 5 by $7\frac{1}{4}$ in. (13 by 19 cm.) for body. Four pieces foam sheeting each 3 by $\frac{1}{2}$ in. (8 by 1·5 cm.) for legs. Two pieces non-fray fabric each $6\frac{1}{2}$ by $1\frac{1}{2}$ in. (16·5 by 4 cm.) for legs. One piece non-fray fabric $5\frac{1}{2}$ by $5\frac{1}{2}$ in. (14 by 14 cm.) for body. One piece foam sheeting $2\frac{1}{2}$ by $\frac{1}{2}$ in. (7 by 1·5 cm.) for neck. Two pieces strong string each 10 in. (25 cm.) long, for arms. One piece non-fray fabric 7 by 2 in. (18 by 5 cm.) for hands. Two plastic bottle tops each $1\frac{1}{4}$ in. (3 cm.) in diameter for feet. One 3 in. (7·5 cm.) polystyrene sphere for head. Two pearl beads.

Weights are required in hands and feet. Use flattened lead shot or small heavy washers.

To make

Follow instructions for making Sue. The pullover is the same as Sue's dress but shorter. Use dotted lines of pattern, Fig. 176.

Trousers

Use piece of non-fray fabric 8 by $7\frac{1}{2}$ in. (20 by 19 cm.).

1. Fold fabric in half and cut up the fold for $6\frac{1}{2}$ in. (16·5 cm.), Fig. 184a.
2. Oversew from A to B for $1\frac{1}{2}$ in. (4 cm.). The right side of the fabric should be inside, Fig. 184b.
3. Open out so that the seam is in the centre and join the fabric to form legs, Fig. 184c. Turn right side out.
4. Put trousers on puppet, pleat at each side of waist and stitch to body, Fig. 184d.

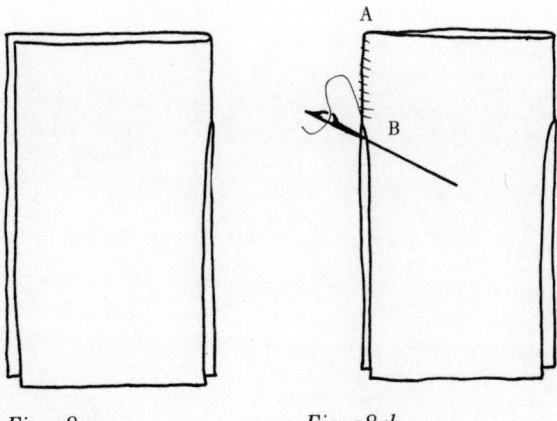

Fig. 184a   *Fig. 184b*

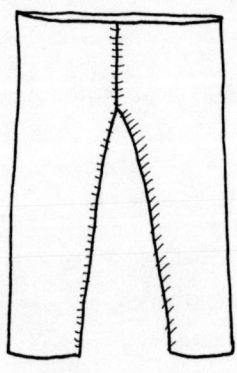

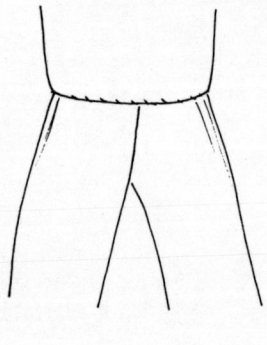

Fig. 184c   Fig. 184d

Electrified Puppets

A puppet can be made so that an electric light can be fitted inside. The light may be shown throughout the performance or it may be used to give signals from the body or head. It must be remembered that the battery used should not be large or heavy, otherwise great strain will be put on the puppet construction and the performer.

Some plastics which are soft and pliable can be cut easily with a knife; thus a section can be cut out of a container or partly cut out and lifted up like a lid. Or perhaps a container may have a lid and wires could easily be brought out through it.

The basic principles for wiring a puppet are given here.

Apparatus   A torch bulb. One torch battery as shown in Fig. 185 or a $4\frac{1}{2}$ V flat battery. Bell wire. Insulating tape.

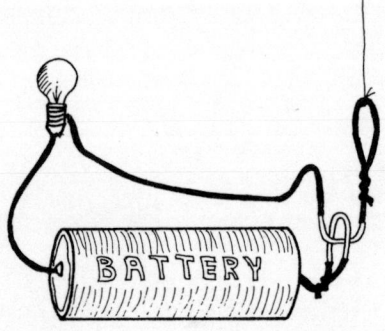

Fig. 185

Method   Bare the ends of the wire. Solder one end to the side of the bulb and the other end to the end of the battery.

Take a shorter piece of flex and bare the ends, soldering one end to the end of the bulb.

Take another short piece of flex and bare the ends, soldering one end to the other end of the battery.

If the two remaining ends are joined together, the bulb will light up, Fig. 185.

The battery should be fitted into a box and padded to keep it firm, Fig. 186. Then it is placed inside the body of the puppet, Fig. 187, and two holes should be made in the lid, one for the bulb and the other for the switch.

A transparent plastic container should be placed over the bulb.

How the switch works is shown in Fig. 185. When the thread is pulled, this causes the two bare wires to meet and complete the circuit. The bulb then lights up.

The puppet can be fairly simple in design because the main interest lies in the lighting. The puppet in Fig. 188 is easily made and the legs are stuck to the body.

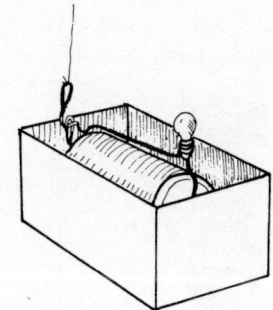

Fig. 186

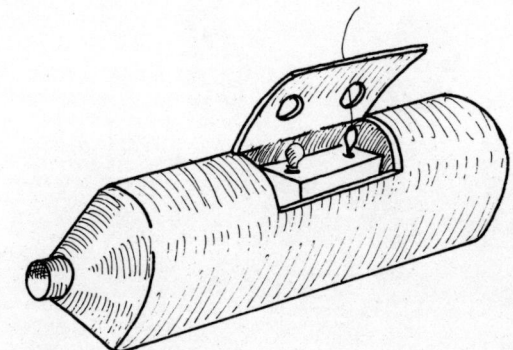

Fig. 187

Fig. 188

Movement and Sound

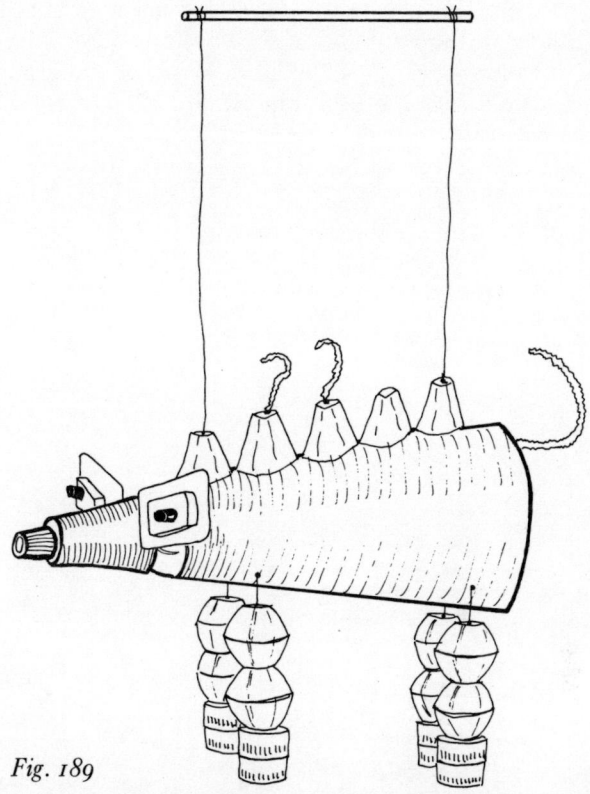

Fig. 189

All marionettes need to be attached to controls to enable them to move and, in certain instances, to make sounds of their own when raised and lowered.

Short-necked creatures
Animals and creatures without long necks should be suspended from one length of thin wood and a thread attached to the rear of the body and also the front, Fig. 189. It may be necessary to burn holes in the body, using a hot needle, so that the threads can be attached. They could also be tied round the neck of the animal. A little adhesive should also be used on the threads to secure to the body.

Long-necked creatures

These should have separate controls, one for the body as for the previous animal, and one for the head. This allows the head to move independently of the body and this flexibility of movement adds greater interest to the character. The head may have two threads, one from each side, as in Luna-Mog. The thread passes under the head and is attached with adhesive. The length of the threads should allow the head to rest on the ground whilst the body is raised, Fig. 190. The piece of wood for this control should be slightly longer than the width of the head. For some creatures, only a single thread is necessary as in Verti-Brek.

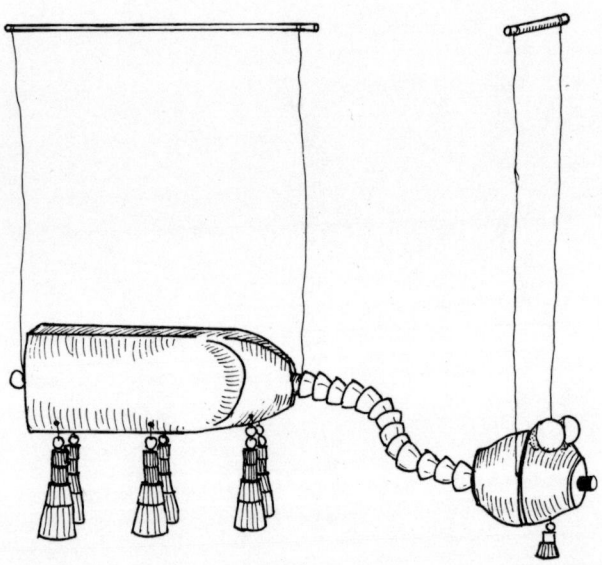

Fig. 190

Speaking creatures

Speaking animals may be used for speech. In Kwok the mouth opens when the jaw thread is lowered, and the head itself is also suspended on a thread, these two threads being attached to the same rod, Fig. 191.

Ele-Lek is also an animal which can make mouth-opening movements. For this the trunk and head are attached to one control.

124

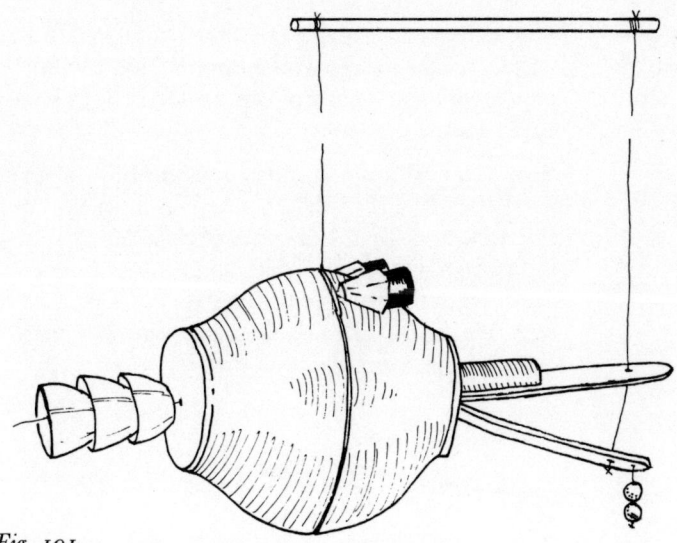

Fig. 191

Creatures with long tails

Tails can give interest in movement and a thread should be attached from the tail to the body control, Fig. 192.

The tail can be operated by the right hand, while the left hand is holding the body control.

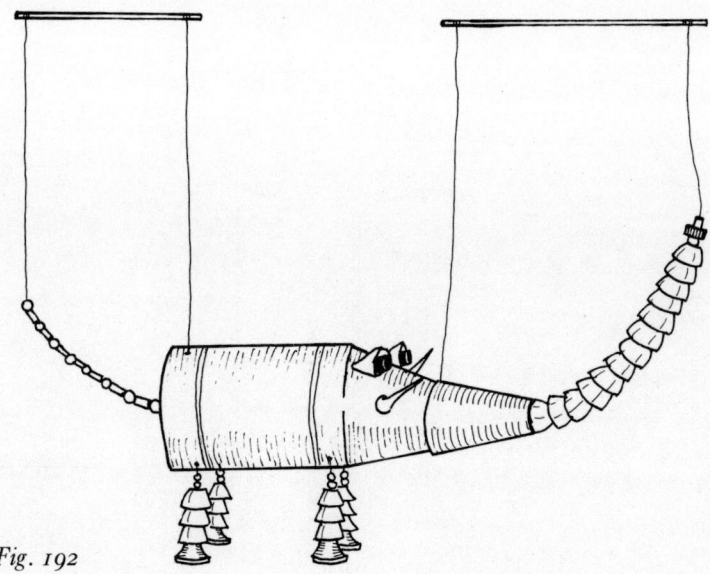

Fig. 192

**The
controls**

The manner in which a creature is attached to a control depends largely on the design of the puppet, and therefore no set method of attaching to a control can be given. It is simply a matter for experiment.

Spy-Lek requires the body to be carefully suspended because of its shape. The threads are attached from the top, each side and the back, Fig. 193. A diagram of the control is shown in Fig. 194, indicating where each part should be attached. The arms are attached to the front of the control or they could be attached to a separate control. In this way, fewer threads need be attached to one control.

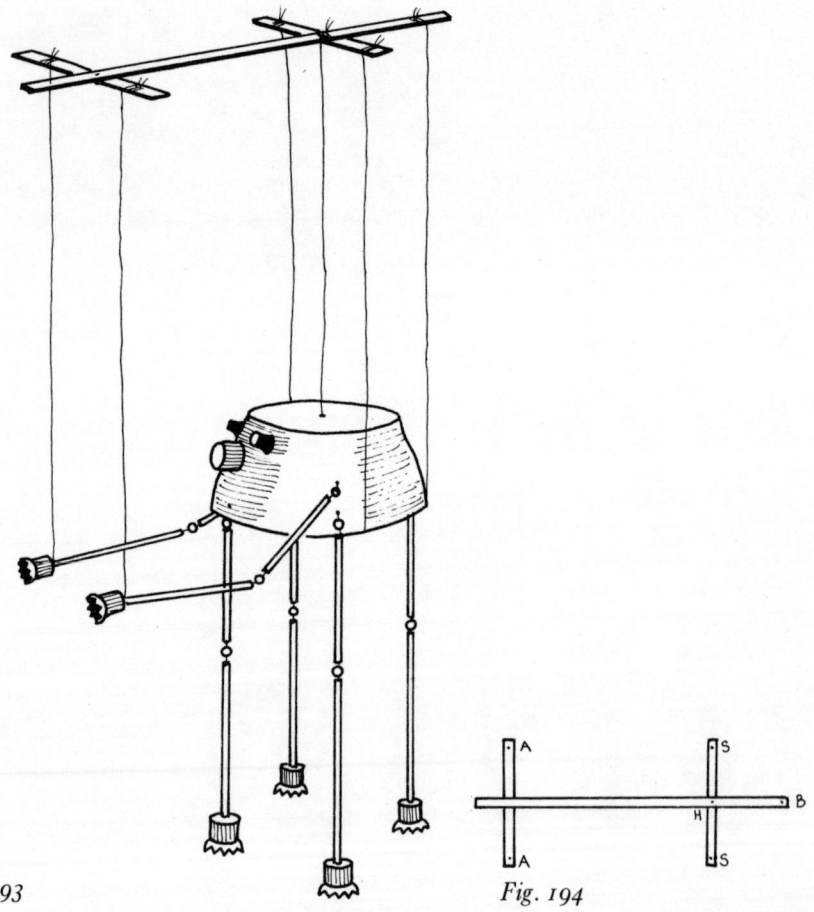

Fig. 193

Fig. 194

The
sounds

The animals or creatures all make interesting sounds which give them an individual character. This happens when the puppet is raised from the ground and lowered again. In the case of the Luna-Mog, the body control can be kept still, while the head control is raised and lowered. The bottle top under the chin makes an interesting sound. It is the flexibility of the neck which enables the animals to make varied and interesting movements. Each creature should be moved round in order to discover what individual movement and sound can be developed, and thus a style of its own can be achieved.

Puppet
People

There are various ways of attaching this type of puppet to a control, according to the movement and simplicity of the strings.

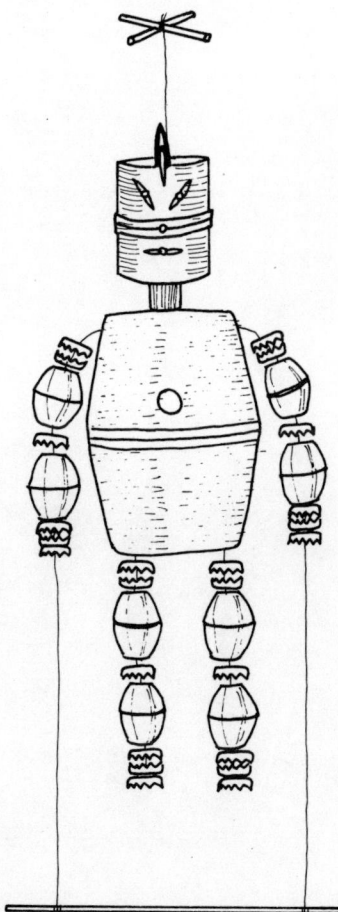

Fig. 195

1. Suspend puppet from the head to a cross bar (made from two pieces of thin wood, each about 4 in. (10 cm.) long, stuck or nailed together). Attach the hands to a separate piece of wood. The threads should be about 24 in. (61 cm.) long, Fig. 195. If several puppets of the same design are to perform as a group, then all head threads should be attached to one control, and all arms to another, so that in performance all the figures make the same kind of movement (see photograph on page 103).

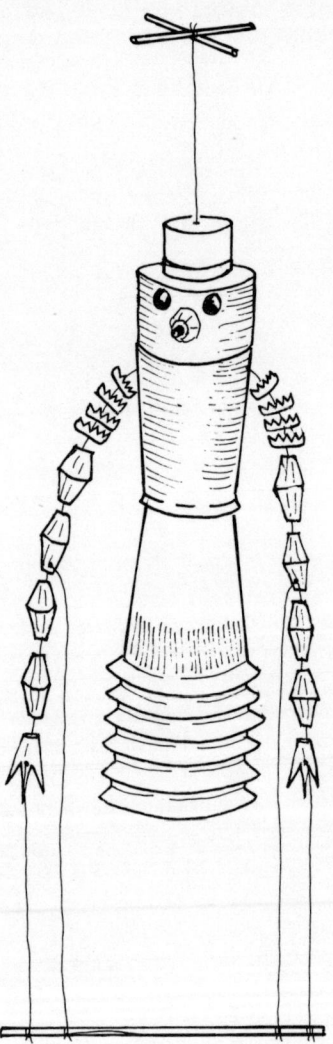

Fig. 196

The Conductor, Fig. 196. The head and hands are attached to separate controls as in Fig. 195 but the elbow joints are also attached by threads to the hand control. This gives a wide variety of movement.

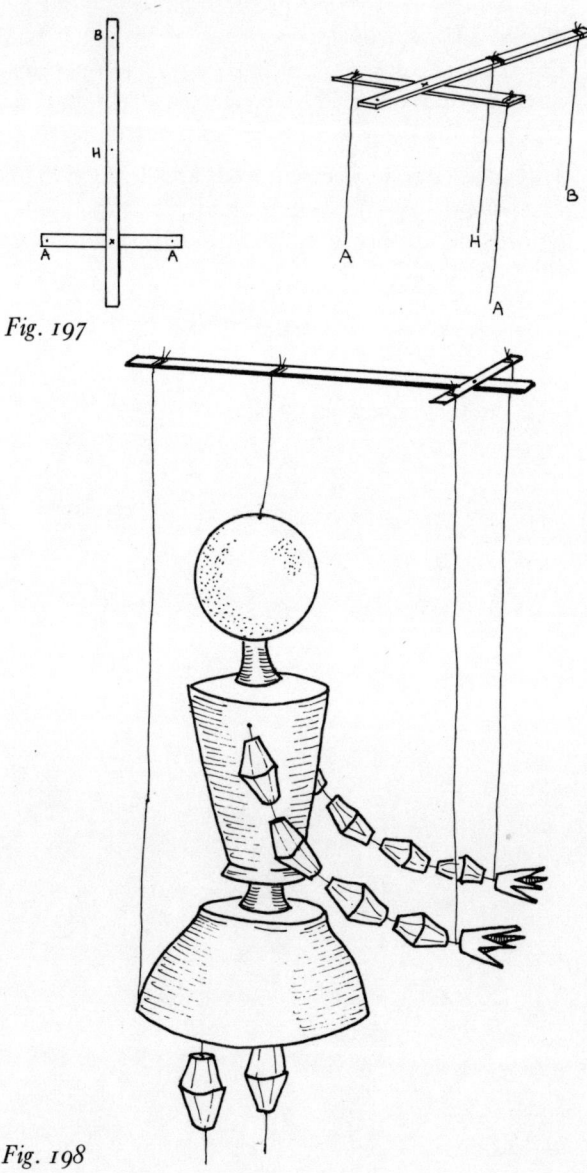

Fig. 197

Fig. 198

2. Make a cross bar, Fig. 197, 9 by 9 in. (23 by 23 cm.). Attach all the strings as in Fig. 198. The arm strings may be attached to the wrist or tips of the hands, according to movements required. If a string is attached to the lower part of the body at the back, this is called the bowing string and is attached to B of Fig. 197. When all strings are adjusted properly then the arms should be straight down and the puppet standing erect. A puppet can perform without a bowing string. Sue on page 109 works quite well without one and it is one less thread to get entangled.

If leg movements are required, attach threads to the knee joint and suspend on a separate rod, Fig. 199. The length of the threads should enable the control to be held at the same height as the body one.

Fig. 199

Performance

Your puppets are finished, but what for? Are they just to lie in a box, or hang on the wall? Or will you bring your creations to life and show your skill as a puppeteer? With a certain amount of practice, by yourself and with others, you should soon be in a position to put on your own "Puppet Show"—your "something from nothing" entertainment.

First, experiment with each puppet to see what kinds of movement it can do. Practise in a mirror, looking at the puppet, not at your hands. Lay it down on the ground, and then gradually bring it to life, moving only one part at a time. Do not jerk the puppet; its actions must flow naturally. Make the most of all the flexible parts of the puppet, so that it gives the impression of being alive. Then move it across the floor, using a variety of movements: crawling, gliding, walking, running, jumping. Can it walk? Can it slide on its tail? This is the time to make any adjustments to the stringing, to remove a string if it is carrying no weight, or to add one to improve the balance. You should also make sure that the strings are the right length for you. You should be able to hold the controls without bending down.

Next try some simple actions: waving hands, clapping, kneeling, dancing, or shaking the head. Always keep the puppet's feet or legs on the ground unless you intend some unusual effect like swinging through the air.

Then get the puppet to speak and sing. Even puppets without actual mouths can do this very well, by moving in time to the most important words. Practise to a short rhyme, then a song, looking in the mirror all the time.

By now you should be getting to know your puppet. Some of the simpler puppets are limited to one type of action, but this can be varied in direction and intensity. Other puppets do all sorts of different things and like human actors are capable of many changes of mood.

Once you have gained confidence in operating the puppet, try one in each hand. Then find a puppet partner and work out a duet sequence. Start some distance apart, spot your partner, run to meet him, embrace, dance and walk away, waving goodbye. Try not to talk to your fellow puppeteer; only communicate through the puppets. Rehearse other situations, and continue to work with a mirror.

When you have become accustomed to working with a partner, form small groups of not more than six puppets. Keep the noise down and be on the alert for your puppet to react to the rest of the group. You might like to play "Puppet Charades", one group at a time. The audience tries to guess the meaning. No speaking is permitted. This not only makes it more amusing, but also develops your powers of manipulation and imagination.

"O'Grady says" works well with puppets. Remember that you only obey the command, "Touch the floor", "Shake your body", etc. when O'Grady says. If the instruction is simply "Touch the floor", you take no notice and continue with what you were doing previously. Any puppet which obeys the wrong order is "out" of the game.

You can make up a group for choral speaking or singing. Memorise a short verse and chant it as you operate the puppets. Number songs are always popular. They are rhythmical and lend themselves to a variety of actions. For example, in "Ten Green Bottles" the appropriate number of puppets can dance as the numbers are called. Place the puppets in different formations, small groups, circles, straight lines, etc. and vary the movements, sometimes dancing on the spot, sometimes advancing towards another line, sometimes moving round in a circle, then breaking off and following a leader. But whatever the movements, there must be times when just one puppet, or a small group, is performing. Only at climaxes should all the puppets move at the same time. The more economical the movement, the more effective the performance will be.

In the preliminary stages the dramatic activity is unrehearsed and spontaneous. Often a topical chant will emerge from a group of you playing together for the first time. Performance takes place on the floor. This means that there are no difficulties over staging and scenery, and you can get used to the idea of acting "in the round".

Once you have become really interested, and wish to perfect a certain sequence, possibly to repeat it in front of an audience, some of the stage directions will have to be written down, and a producer appointed.

When you come to work out longer items for a show you will find that words and music give an added stimulus to your ideas. Your puppets will send you rushing to the library to search out suitable verse, often descriptive or narrative. But don't worry if your puppets are not completely realistic. For example, any creatures can act out the characters of the whiting, snail, porpoise, lobsters and turtles from "The Lobster Quadrille". The puppets must act out the main outline of the story and only illustrate the detail if they can really do so well. In any performance using words, either said or sung, the diction must be crystal clear; otherwise the meaning will be lost. If the puppets themselves are making so much noise that the words cannot be heard, you can deaden the sound by putting down newspapers or a piece of old carpet for the puppets to walk on. The speakers or singers might if necessary be amplified, provided the sound does not distort.

Here is an example of a song which suits the puppets.

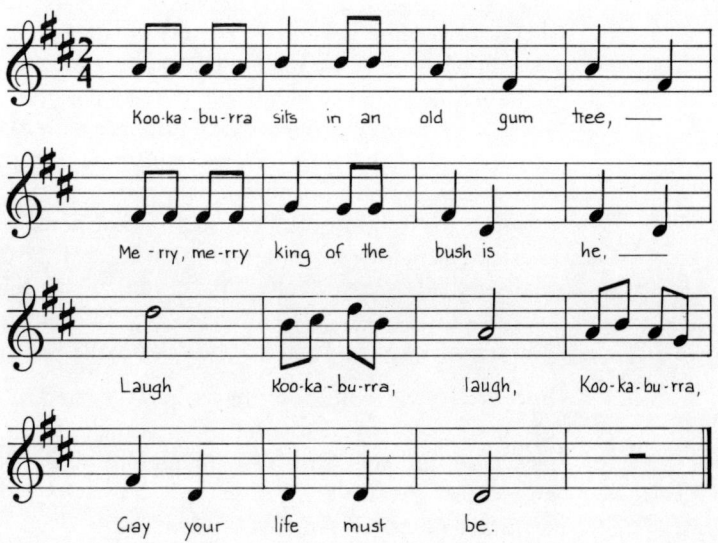

First of all sing the song over. Then let the puppets join in, tapping out the rhythm of the words or swaying quietly to the music. Next, try the puppets by themselves, without the music, to see if the rhythm has been grasped. Avoid speeding up at the end. The song can now be performed in a variety of ways, using contrasting groups and formations.

1. One group acts out the song, while the rest, placed in a semi-circle, create an accompaniment from the rhythm of "Laugh, kookaburra, laugh, kookaburra". For a repeat of the song all the puppets join together in a long line, moving forwards and backwards.
2. Everybody performs "Kookaburra" as a round, in two, three, or four parts, with each group moving in a circle.
3. Everybody performs in a ternary (three-part) form. First time through, singing and moving; second time, moving only; third time, singing and moving.
4. Soloists alternate with the full company in a rondo form. First time through, all together, singing and moving; second time, soloist, singing and moving; third time, all together, whistling and moving; fourth time, soloist, moving only; final time, all together, singing and moving off in a long line.

If your musicians can join in the performance, so much the better. Leave plenty of scope for improvisation and solo work, and aim at involving as many of the puppets as possible. Any puppets, human, or animal, could dance to "Kookaburra". Folk-song ballads and sea-shanties are very useful. A separate choir or soloist can sing while the puppets interpret the words. Sometimes, as in "Oh, no John", which can be acted by puppets Sue and Jim, one side can sing the boy's side and the other the girl's. Many ballads are possible. Try "Frankie and Johnny", "Villikins and his Dinah", "Shenandoah", "Widdicombe Fair", etc. You might also like to write your own ballad.

For group activities nothing could be better than Country Dancing or Square Dancing. This is really a form of organised play. We find that with just the right amount of guidance the puppeteers greatly enjoy this type of activity, which also gives scope for plenty of improvised dancing.

This is how we use the traditional dance, Galopede, with our puppets.

The couples make a longways set for not more than four couples. At A1 the two lines dance towards one another, then back. They then cross over, passing their partner on the right and ending up on the opposite side. At the repeat of the music, A2, they go through the same motions, ending where they originally started. At B the puppets and their partners improvise a dance on the spot. At C the first couple moves down from the top to the bottom of the set while the rest go "bang, bang, bang" in time to the music and move up one place. The dance continues until the first couple is back where it started. (Further information about Country Dancing can be obtained from The English Folk Dance and Song Society, Cecil Sharp House, 2 Regent's Park Road, London N.W.1.)

Whenever you use recorded music with your puppets, you must choose carefully. It is generally better to put the music on to tape, and careful use of the pause button and the fading-out control will give you music of the right length. Remember that just one puppet, performing simple actions, cannot possibly keep anyone interested for more than two or three minutes at a time.

You can often find just the right music for an individual puppet.

For example, I like to use "The Elephant" from *The Carnival of the Animals* with Ele-Lek. The three girls, dressed as Yum-Yum, Peep-Bo and Pitti-Sing can dance to "Three Little Maids from School Are We" from *The Mikado*. The Maxi-Aut can exhibit his stupendous technique with a great show of hands at either the opening of the Tchaikovsky Piano Concerto, or the Chopin A Major Prelude. The Conductor can beat time to any music. Arrange for him to walk on to recorded applause. He can then conduct, say, the Radetsky March as the other puppets parade to it.

Kwok is able to sing almost anything, but his rather grotesque attitude suits music which you would not normally expect such a creature to sing. I have used "O for the wings of a dove". Also the 1929 Louis Armstrong recording of "Ain't misbehavin'".

Sue and Jim will fit most pop songs provided a sufficient variety of situations and movements has been worked out. It is often as well to start the music before the puppet appears and to have a chorus for visual and dramatic effect.

The Ballet Dancer has a vast repertoire to choose from. Here again, a solo dance will appear monotonous unless it is well planned. Experiment with *corps de ballet* formations. We have used up to ten small puppets on one control in ballet music, sometimes making a tap-dance effect and sometimes swinging in the air in time to the music. Needless to say, great care in operating a set of puppets like this is essential; otherwise, tangled strings will be the result.

Interest in puppet-making often stimulates creative activity in other directions. These three poems were written by second- and third-year children of Clint Road Junior School, Boys' Department, Liverpool.

Mark Whittaker
LUNER - MOG

Planet Z what a place to be
With the Luner - Mog and the
Red Lek
The Luner - Mog is slow
When he males
he rattles with Joy
Just like a toy
shufeling every Were
his bright eyes atract every - one
you heard clip clop clip - clop
thats the Luner - Mog
Theres the Red - Lek
heavy fearse
and wild
he dosent bounce
he walks like a human being
hes not very fat and his
body works it's self

ALAN CALVERT

THE LUNA MOG

The luna mog is not a dog
A puppy, or a mouse.
It's plastic tops,
And bits of mops,
That you find around the house.

DAVID KNIGHT

THE PUPPETS FROM PUPPET LAND

In the streets of puppet land there
always dancing, jumping and singing.
They go rustling about clip-et-e-clop as
they go along. Some of them fly, some of
them die, broken in pieces splatered to death.

Some of them fight, some of them bite, and
some are just normal, just like me.

The poems could be used in a performance by being read against a background of soft, improvised music which would then continue as a puppet danced to it. You yourself might not be musically inclined but you should ask your musicians to improvise *ostinati* (patterns) in a Pentatonic scale, e.g. C D E G A, or to work within a chord sequence, e.g. G, Emi, C, D$_7$. Wherever possible you should try using live music. This makes a performance as a whole so much more vital. If you are badly equipped for musical instruments you will get valuable help on making your own in Peter Williams's *Lively Craft Cards, Set 2, Making Musical Instruments* (published by Mills & Boon).

When you start making up your own puppet plays, you will have to decide how much should be improvised and how much written down, memorised and acted in the same way each time. The operator can speak the part of his own puppet (this is more interesting) or another group can do the speaking. At all times words must be audible, and the meaning must be clear to the audience. The flow of the drama will be helped by having a variety of sequences, singing, speaking, dancing, audience participation, off-stage action accompanied by music or sound effects, etc. Any awkward gaps in the action can be covered by linking music, and if you have this on a separate tape-recorder you will avoid backstage muddle.

This is the plot of an improvised drama made up by College students. It was performed in the round to an audience of over a hundred young children.

Space Drama

Characters: Two astronauts (earth people)
Two space guards
A mechanic
Space animals and other "people"

Props: One space-craft
One space-chart—floating

The scene is a deserted planet in space. A lone space-craft is circling high in the sky. On it are two astronauts. The craft is in trouble. Lights flash and it shudders, falling towards the ground; crash-landing. (This sequence is accompanied by improvised music and sound effects.)

138

The two astronauts are shaken, but soon recover and start to discuss their predicament. Where are they? Is the planet inhabited? Fortunately, as they are talking, a space-chart floats by and they are able to see that they are quite close to a space-port. They decide to walk to it and set out, floating in the air from time to time because of the lack of gravity.

As they approach the space-port a guard comes out. They run away in fear, only to bump right into another. They beg for help, and after the guard has heard their story he becomes most friendly and helpful, sends for a mechanic to mend their space-craft and invites them to sit down and watch the parade of the space animals, taking their morning exercise. (Improvised music as the animals and their keepers march on.) The astronauts return the compliment by showing the planet-dwellers an earth dance (e.g. "My Grandfather's Clock"). Then the mechanic comes to say that the space-craft is mended. The astronauts exchange goodbyes with all their new friends, and board the space-craft. All the puppets, together with the audience, join in singing "Auld Lang Syne" as the space-craft circles round and then floats away.

Most performances will be for your friends only and will take place on the floor. If you intend putting on a show, or "Puppet Cabaret", performance in the round is still possible and, indeed, preferable in many instances. Make certain, though, that the audience has a good view. Either the performers or the spectators must be raised up. The visual effect is greatly improved if the puppets are used against a black backcloth. The puppeteers should dress in black: black stockings, tights or trousers, with black tunics or cardigans. Black gloves or mitts can be worn and the strings and controls can also be painted black. One or two spotlights on the puppets will really make them show up, particularly if you fade the lights in and out.

If you can borrow drama staging blocks, arrange them to form interesting levels. A group could then perform a dance going round in a circle, walking behind the blocks and performing on them.

Every public performance should be properly organised, both front of stage and behind the scenes. You must think up some way to store the puppets when they are not in use. If hooks are put on the controls the puppets can then be hung up.

You will get endless fun out of making these puppets and creating performances with them. By rehearsing and perfecting your own puppet shows you will bring great pleasure to yourself, your friends and your audiences. There is something of the actor in each one of us—"all the world's a stage"; and through our performing toys, our puppets, we can play out our different parts.

IAN SHARP

Acknowledgements

I am most grateful for the help given to me by those who have been so kind in collecting junk; and to the schools who have allowed me to try out ideas, or who have invited me to see the work done by the children.

I am also grateful to Ian Sharp, Lecturer in Music at St Katharine's College, Liverpool, for discovering so many possibilities in the movements of these creatures and for developing these ideas into an exciting brand of performance.

The three poems in the Performance section were written by second- and third-year children of Clint Road Junior School, Boys' Department, Liverpool (Class Teacher: Mr C. Roberts). The poems are reproduced by kind permission of the Chief Education Officer, City of Liverpool.

I wish to thank Christopher Roberts for his work with the line illustrations in the book. The silhouette illustrations were done by the author.

Mrs J. Johnstone, who is always so good at deciphering my handwriting, has finally enabled my work to go into print.